MW00480453

WHAT PEOPLE ARE SAYING ABOUT
9 DISCIPLINES OF ENDURING LEADERSHIP . . .

"This book will change your life. Dr. Kent Ingle makes leadership accessible to everyone—no matter if you're established or just getting started. This isn't a book full of Christian vocabulary and insider language. This is real talk about real change in a way that you can get excited about. This needs to be the next book you read!"

—MARK BATTERSON
New York Times bestselling author and lead pastor of
National Community Church, Washington, DC

"It's one thing to have potential. It's another thing to experience it. The first requires insight, the second requires discipline. In his new book, *9 Disciplines of Enduring Leadership,* Kent Ingle gives you the tools you need to live life to the full."

—ROBERT CROSBY
author of *The One Jesus Loves*

"*9 Disciplines of Enduring Leadership* reminds readers that success is derived in quiet moments of personal resolve. It's too easy to accept the status quo and believe your present circumstances are the best they will ever be. That simply isn't true. If you have a nagging feeling you need a renewed approach to life, this book will help you make that fundamental shift."

—WILFREDO DE JESÚS
senior pastor, New Life Covenant Church, Chicago, IL, and author of *In the Gap* and *Amazing Faith*

"Here's a book by a man who wasn't given much of a chance to win. Yet in a few short years Kent Ingle assembled a team of "no name" champions to build the strongest "culture" in a university I've ever witnessed. He records in the pages of *9 Disciplines of Enduring Leadership* the foundational principles on which he accomplished such a daunting task."

—RICH WILKERSON, SR.
pastor, Trinity Church, Miami, FL

"Dr. Ingle has lived what he writes, which means you can trust that what you read comes from real life experiences. Because of Dr. Ingle's passion and personal example, many leaders have already been tremendously impacted, and I know that from reading this book you will be impacted too."

—LUKE SHEMETH
Southeastern University, student body president

9
DISCIPLINES
OF ENDURING
LEADERSHIP

DEVELOPING THE POTENTIAL
OF YOUR DIVINE DESIGN

KENT INGLE

Copyright © 2015 by Kent Ingle
ALL RIGHTS RESERVED.

Published by Influence Resources
1445 North Boonville Avenue
Springfield, Missouri 65802

No portion of this book may be reproduced, stored in a
retrieval system, or transmitted in any form or by any
means—electronic, mechanical, photocopy, recording, or
any other—except for brief quotations in printed reviews,
without the prior written permission of the publisher.

Collaboration and Developmental Editing: Ben Stroup
(www.benstroup.com)—Greenbrier, TN
Cover design by Plain Joe Studios (www.plainjoestudios.com)
Interior design by Prodigy Pixel (www.prodigypixel.com)

Unless otherwise specified, Scripture quotations used in this
book are taken from the 2011 edition of the Holy Bible, New
International Version®. NIV®. Copyright © 1973, 1978, 1984,
2011 by Biblica, Inc. ™ Used by permission of Zondervan. All
rights reserved worldwide.www.zondervan.com. The "NIV" and
"New International Version" are trademarks registered in the
United States Patent and Trademark Office by Biblica, Inc.™
Scripture quotations marked (NKJV) are taken from The
New King James version®. © 1982 by Thomas Nelson,
Inc. Used by permission. All rights reserved.

ISBN: 978-1-62912-170-3
Printed in the United States of America
18 17 16 15 • 1 2 3 4 5

CONTENTS

FOREWORD

I've seen and studied leadership from the c-suite to the highest elected offices of government and everywhere in between. I've met leaders who surprised me, leaders who inspired me, and a few who shocked me. I've written more than eight books on leadership, given countless seminars and keynotes, and continue to write a variety of columns and articles for a number of publications. There is one thing that is consistent among every leader I've ever observed: they understand the power of personal discipline.

Leadership doesn't just happen; it's not an accident. It's the product of years of commitment, tough decisions, careful choices, and hard work. Leaders are refined by difficult situations and propelled forward by successful ones. But none of that happens without a lifestyle of discipline.

Many would-be leaders perceive discipline to be a burden and a limiting factor in their lives and leadership. Nothing could be further from the truth! It's personal discipline that helps them reach new heights of influence, recognition, and success. It's not just what you do on the public stage that makes you successful. Rather, it's what you do in the quiet moments when no one is watching that will make or break your legacy.

Dr. Kent Ingle is someone who has experienced a great deal of success in his life in a variety of contexts. It's his decision to bring his life into alignment with his faith, principles, and experience that continues to expand his reach and multiply his impact. It would have been easy for Dr. Ingle to rest in the moment of his present success, yet he continues to lean into his current role and take the organization he leads to new heights. I can only imagine the number of people looking to Dr. Ingle right now trying to figure out the formula to his success. I'll tell you: it's personal and professional discipline.

I teach leaders about the role of MVPs in their success. You're probably thinking about a phrase often associated with athletics. I'm actually talking about a different type of MVP: Most Valuable and Profitable Activities. The decisions we make that are valuable and profitable are the very activities that will lead us to the outcomes we desire. But life is rarely that straightforward or simple in real time. In fact, the greater your success, the more you can count on opportunities for distraction to come. The only way to overcome the challenge of focus is to do your MVPs on a daily basis.

You have a choice to make: will you choose to align your behavior with your values, or will you choose to chase every opportunity, respond to every email, and answer every request? One will unlock your leadership potential. The other will keep you so busy that you'll never come close to achieving your potential impact. If I had to sum up the path to real leadership in one word, it would be *discipline*. This book will show you in a practical way how it will change your leadership and your life and set you up for a legacy of success.

—MARK SANBORN
Scuba Diver, Motorcycle Rider, Cancer Survivor, Husband, Dad, *New York Times* Bestselling Author, and Professional Speaker

MY WAKE-UP CALL

———————

Y ou have sugar diabetes, and it's bad."

That's not what I expected to hear. I knew I was overweight, but I never thought my health and my life were in danger. My blood sugar count was over 350 mg/dl (milligrams per deciliter)—normal, before meals, is around 100 mg/dl. I was 250 too high!

The doctor's words rippled through my mind. I was a ticking time bomb! According to the Mayo Clinic, high blood sugar can cause heart attack, stroke, vision problems, nerve damage, kidney problems, and gum disease. I was on a fast track to one or more of these debilitating conditions. How did I get here, and what was I going to do about it?

I knew there were short-term solutions to the problem, but I wanted more than that. I didn't want to become dependent on medications to manage my irresponsibility. I needed to become more self-disciplined if I was going to win the battle against my own bad habits. I was stuck in a dangerous cycle that could eventually kill me. Something had to change, and the change had to be permanent.

My "aha" moment had far-reaching repercussions. I started thinking about the stewardship of life and how it is my responsibility to manage everything God has entrusted to me. That includes my health but also my time, talents, resources, influence, leadership, family, and other components of life.

I never planned to be irresponsible regarding my health; it happened over time when I failed to pay attention to what was really important.

Life can't be separated into disconnected silos; the parts are all linked. That might not seem like a deep spiritual truth. Honestly, it's not deep, but it is foundational. Life really is interconnected, and we all have the responsibility to manage it according to God's divine design. Leadership is all about faithfully exercising our minds, bodies, influence, and all that God has given us.

Nowhere in the Bible does God commend a lack of discipline. Nowhere in the Bible does God tell us that we are better able to serve Him when we let our habits take control of our lives. That's not in the Bible, but it's how many of us live. I know because I tried it.

When we understand how interconnected life is, we recognize the importance of discipline. Discipline is "the systematic management of your life to prepare and position you for your divine design." Discipline and stewardship are one and the same. Discipline brings order to life and is absolutely required if we're going to be good stewards of the call to leadership.

We must pay a price to get to the next level of any pursuit in life. Millions of high school students participate in sports, but only a small fraction of them ever make it to the professional level. You need more than natural talent. Making it to the next level requires dedication and determination. For leaders, this truth is ever present.

When my whole life is in order, things come into alignment, and if I am learning and growing, I won't have to fear getting "stuck." I'll experience the truth of Romans 12:2 where Paul says, "Do not conform to the pattern of this world, but be transformed by the renewing of your mind. Then you will be able to test and approve what God's will is—his good, pleasing and perfect will."

The Greek word translated *renewing* derives from the word that means *renovate.* If you've watched a home improvement show, you've seen renovation at work. Professionals go into a home and decide what to keep, what to reuse, and what to replace. Similarly, when God begins transforming our thought processes, we allow Him to renovate our lives. He will show us what to keep, what to reuse, and what to replace. That's how the Holy Spirit works.

When the notion of becoming more self-disciplined hit me, though, I didn't need to add something to my to-do list. *I needed a renovation.* I needed God to change the way I thought because every action is preceded by a mental process. When my thinking is aligned with God's principles, my actions have a better chance of aligning with Him. That's what I wanted, but I knew it wouldn't happen if I didn't take action.

This wasn't the first time I encountered my own faulty thinking, and, honestly, it won't be the last. Faulty thinking is at the core of many things we accept as "normal" today. If we aren't allowing the Holy Spirit to continually renovate our minds, we will follow cultural trends and compromise our divine design and calling.

Many believers are in a spiritual crisis that parallels the physical crisis I experienced. They never intended for things to get out of control. They never saw the warning signs. They simply drifted toward spiritual lethargy without any point of reference to guide them.

You have a spiritual problem, and it's bad might be the words that help you see the need for self-discipline in your life, and that's what this book is about. I don't claim to have all the answers, but I do know what God has been doing in my own life. I know His divine design for each of us is to live amazing lives that give us a sense of meaning and purpose while drawing attention to His grace and love. You can't fulfill God's destiny without discipline.

In the nine chapters that follow, I introduce you to nine disciplines that will help you discover and activate your divine design. These disciplines require sacrifice and focus. You'll be challenged to reconsider your thinking processes in light of God's desire that you be an effective steward of everything He has entrusted to you.

It's not enough to discover your divine design; you must also *do* something with it. Through the intentional application of these disciplines, your life will be transformed, and the best version of you will be unveiled.

What are the nine disciplines?

1.   The discipline of self-awareness

2.   The discipline of self-management

3.   The discipline of self-preparedness

4.   The discipline of character

5.   The discipline of relationships

6. The discipline of generosity

7. The discipline of learning

8. The discipline of opportunity

9. The discipline of missional living

Each of these disciplines is connected to the others, so by the end of this book, you will have a comprehensive life system and strategy for igniting your passion and living up to the incredible potential God has placed in you.

You might be a young person thinking about college. You might be a young parent with concerns for the environment in which you'll raise your children. You could be an empty nester with the desire to come alive in the second half of life. No matter where you are, these nine disciplines will help you tap into God's plan and will point you toward His divine design for your life.

The psalmist said it best:

For you created my inmost being; you knit me together in my mother's womb. I praise you because I am fearfully and wonderfully made; your works are wonderful, I know that full well. My frame was not hidden from you when I was made in the secret place, when I was woven together in the depths of the earth. Your eyes saw my unformed body; all the days ordained for me were written in your book before one of them came to be (Psalm 139:13–16).

God knew you before anyone else realized you existed. He put you together according to His plan for your life, and the closer you are to Him, the better you will understand His plan.

Too many people try to live according to their own plans. They decide what they want to do and then invite God along on their journeys, but that's not how it works. God will never compromise His perfect plan. He will never settle for mediocrity when excellence is possible. He will never sanction our plans as a substitute for His. C. S. Lewis said, "God cannot give us a happiness and peace apart from Himself, because it is not there. There is no such thing."

THE DISCIPLINE OF
SELF-AWARENESS

"DON'T COMPROMISE YOURSELF.
YOU'RE ALL YOU'VE GOT."
—*JANIS JOPLIN*

Self-assessments are everywhere. In a few clicks online, you can discover all kinds of interesting things about yourself. Some of those "discoveries" are restatements of obvious traits. Others are a little more surprising.

Whether using an assessment tool or other means, the discipline of self-awareness is possible. We often understand who we are by evaluating our experiences. The old adage says, "Experience is the best teacher." Some people attribute the saying to Benjamin Franklin, others to Thomas Taylor. It most likely originated as a Latin proverb, but regardless of its origin, it seems incomplete. We don't learn simply by going through an experience; we learn when we reflect on that experience. *Reflection produces self-awareness.*

At any moment, you are going through several experiences simultaneously. In addition to your professional responsibilities, you are engaged in other activities both physical and mental. Have you ever stopped and asked what it's like to encounter you in each of these settings? This is a great way to become more self-aware.

At the end of each day, I like to reflect on that day's experiences. What individuals did I meet? What did I learn? How did I respond? Whom did I lead, and how effective was my leadership influence? You might have other questions to add. The key to beneficial reflection is to look back from a neutral perspective and replay the experiences as if watching them on television.

As I look back on my experiences, I gain a new appreciation or awareness of my gifts and abilities and how effectively I used them. At times, I see myself letting my divine design influence the way I use my gifts. At other times, I allow my gifts and my design to get disconnected. Yet I would never know that if I didn't reflect on my experiences.

AWARENESS OF YOUR GIFTS

Everyone has natural talents and abilities, but spiritual gifts are a byproduct of a relationship with Christ. Living up to your full potential can't be accomplished by relying on talents alone. Because God designed and created you, His design includes a need to rely on His presence. The Holy Spirit's presence in your life takes you far beyond your talent and skill. It forces you to acknowledge the favor of God.

Although there are a number of tools available to help you discern your talents, you probably are already aware of your natural abilities. What do you know you do well? What do others say you do well? The answers to these questions will give you a clue about your talents.

But how can you know your gifts? Gifts are what you can do as a result of God's Spirit living inside and through you. There usually is no explanation for your gifting. Some people say gifts are supernatural, and they are right. Your spiritual gifts are the avenues through which God works to bring honor and glory to Himself. While your natural talents and abilities can help make *you* famous, your gifts make *God* famous.

We sometimes struggle to acknowledge our gifts because we don't want to appear arrogant or boastful. That's certainly noble. However, our Creator gave each of us a unique set of gifts that

> When you work outside your area of giftedness, at least two people suffer: you and the person who really should be doing that task.

He wants us to use. You should be able to distinguish between your talents and abilities and your gifts. You had your talents and abilities before you had a relationship with God. He can also re-purpose your talents for His purposes.

Being aware of what you are gifted to do will help you identify those aspects of your work that should be delegated. As a leader, you have the responsibility to use your gifts efficiently and to provide opportunities for the people you lead to use their gifts as well. When you work outside your area of giftedness, at least two people suffer: you and the person who really should be doing that task. You suffer because it takes you longer to do things you aren't gifted to do. Sure, you might be able to do the task, but is there someone better equipped to do it? Other people suffer because they are denied the chance to express their giftedness in the best way.

When you are aware of how you employ your gifts, you will be aware of how you allow others to employ their gifts. When people are allowed to put their gifts to work, they will be more satisfied in their roles within our organizations. Satisfied people are more productive, creative, and positive. Dissatisfied people demonstrate the opposite.

God's will is always found in your DNA. You find it as you look within and unlock your divine design. When you understand your design, you will have a better understanding of how God wants to use you. It is vital that leaders set aside time to inventory and reflect on their gifts in light of their current situations.

SELF-ASSESSMENT TESTS

You've probably taken one or more self-assessments such as the DiSC® Profile, StrengthsFinder, or the Myers-Briggs Type Indicator®. These assessments are industry standards that have been and continue to be helpful in almost every aspect of life. They are intended to increase self-awareness and help us better interact with others.

Every assessment, however, should be viewed subjectively in light of the conditions present when you complete the assessment. Stress, fatigue, and current events all have the potential to affect your responses. Assessments like the ones mentioned above are designed to compensate for variances in your responses, but if you took an assessment ten years ago, your responses might have changed.

Many leaders find it beneficial to encourage their team members to take self-assessments in order to identify the best strategies for communication, interaction, and functionality. Self-assessment tools offer the objective evaluation we need for our teams and our leadership.

DiSC can help you be more productive and improve communication and collaboration. It can help you and your team address personality differences so you can function more efficiently and effectively. The DiSC Profile will help you recognize how you respond to conflict, what causes you stress, your problem-solving strategies, and the things that motivate you. The more you understand about yourself, the better you'll be able to lead your team and maximize its effectiveness by minimizing interpersonal conflict.

StrengthsFinder by Tom Rath is an online assessment and printed resource that helps people discover and utilize their personal strengths. It is built on the understanding that many people spend a great portion of their lives trying to improve their weaknesses rather than capitalizing on their strengths. StrengthsFinder distinguishes your strengths and weaknesses and provides practical steps to maximize your personal strengths in your leadership role.

The Myers-Briggs Type Indicator measures your psychological type and how you view life. The sixteen personality types are based on the work of psychologist Carl Jung and have been used in personal, academic, and professional settings to help better understand how an individual might function in any given environment.

Some people argue that self-awareness is a New Age philosophy and, therefore, should be avoided, but that's not true. As a believer, your self-image is a reflection of Christ, and your personality, giftedness, and contribution to the world are expressions of the Holy Spirit's presence in your life. When you pursue self-awareness, you are simply tapping into God's divine design.

Self-awareness isn't about elevating yourself or seeking personal gain. The better you understand how you are put together, the better equipped you'll be to lead. When you are self-aware, you are poised to step into the role God has for you. Your design and your task will fit together nicely.

In Acts 17:16–33, we see an example of what happens when people reconcile their lives with their divine design. As he traveled around Athens, Paul noticed the religious bent of its citizens. He saw idols representing a number of gods and even found an idol dedicated to an unknown god.

Self-awareness positions us to help other people.

Though acclaimed for their knowledge, the Greeks were afraid they might have left out a god, so they created a spare.

Paul was aware of his giftedness and God's Spirit in his life. He was confident that he could help the Greek philosophers understand their search for significance and their need for a relationship with the only true God. Because Paul understood himself, he was able to help others.

Self-awareness positions us to help other people. Until we understand who we are, we will never be able to help others know who they are. Self-awareness will help you know what you should and should not be doing. For example, when a job opportunity comes your way, being self-aware will help you make the right decision as to your gift mix for that position. When you aren't self-aware, you will waste a lot of time doing things that should be done by others.

We all want to be good at what we do. No one sets out to be mediocre. Self-awareness tunes your life to your strengths, and as you cultivate and utilize your strengths, you'll experience authentic peace and joy. You will come alive in ways you never dreamed possible.

There is no way you can live in the center of God's will without cultivating the discipline of self-awareness. You'll learn more about who God is as you learn more about how He designed you. The discipline of self-awareness is one of the most important steps in the process of becoming the leader you were designed to be.

KEY IDEAS

- We don't learn simply by going through an experience; we learn when we reflect on it. *Reflection produces self-awareness.*

- The key to beneficial reflection is to be willing to look back from a neutral perspective and replay the experiences as if you were watching them on television.

- As a leader, you have the responsibility to use your gifts efficiently and to provide opportunities for those you lead to use their gifts as well.

- When you understand your design, you will have a better understanding of how God wants to use you.

- Until we understand who we are, we will never be able to help others know who they are.

DISCUSSION QUESTIONS

1. What are two or three things you have learned from recent experiences?

2. Think about a situation in which you were involved. Replay it in your mind as if you were outside of the situation, watching it happen. What conclusions would you draw by observing yourself?

3. Consider your daily activities. Which of your gifts do you use most efficiently? Which do you use inefficiently? Why do you use some gifts more efficiently than others?

4. What are some things God has accomplished through you? What did you learn about yourself and God in those experiences?

5. How are you helping others discover who they are? What is your strategy for encouraging or mentoring those entrusted to you?

YOUR NEXT STEP

1. If you haven't already done so, identify and complete one of the self-assessments mentioned in this chapter.

2. Arrange to spend time with someone who shares a good relationship with you. Ask that person to help you identify ways you can better use your gifts.

3. Use the journal at the end of the book to record your thoughts as you allow God to work through your life.

THE DISCIPLINE OF
SELF-MANAGEMENT

"IF TIME BE OF ALL THINGS THE MOST
PRECIOUS, WASTING TIME MUST BE THE
GREATEST PRODIGALITY."
—*BENJAMIN FRANKLIN*

Twenty-four hours. One thousand four hundred and forty minutes. Eighty-six thousand four hundred seconds. One day. Once spent, time can never be reclaimed. We often look back on time wasted with a sense of regret, and we celebrate time well used. Time is one of our most precious resources. It is no respecter of social status or affluence. The rich and the poor all get the same twenty-four hours.

Time, however, isn't the only commodity we have to manage. We've been entrusted with all of life—the spiritual, physical, and emotional. In Matthew 22:37, Jesus said, "Love the Lord your God with all your heart and with all your soul and with all your mind." This encompasses every aspect of life. We've been entrusted with amazing resources that should be used in accordance with the wishes of the One who entrusted them to us.

If any part of your life is out of sync, this will affect the other parts. Emotional stress can have physical consequences. Physical limitations can affect your emotions. You get the idea. If we are going to fulfill our divine designs, we must pay attention to all the important aspects of our lives. We can't be at our best unless we make self-management a priority.

Life balance is the key to long-term success. You must learn to manage your time as well as your health and intellect. Although you probably already have a lot of information about each of these areas, I want to talk about them in light of our God-given responsibility to manage life according to His plan.

THE BODY

We don't really have to get into a philosophical discussion about the importance of exercise. We all know that age and diet often work against us. Sometimes, the harder we work at our jobs and life responsibilities, the more brutal we are on our bodies. I understand. Physical exercise, however, is critical to an overall life balance. Thirty minutes of exercise each day will make a big difference in how you feel and in how you perform.

Start with something simple like a walk around your neighborhood, or get a DVD with beginner cardiovascular exercises or yoga. Although you might have been a star athlete in your younger years, don't overestimate your current physical prowess. Start slowly, and work at a pace that pushes you but won't cause injury.

You also need to think about what you eat. If you consume more calories than you burn, you will gain weight. If you burn more calories than you consume, you will lose weight. Make sure you get enough protein and vegetables. Limit your consumption of sugar and white carbohydrates. View food as fuel for the life you want to live. Good fuel produces a healthy life; bad fuel leads to a number of problems including obesity, type 2 diabetes, cardiovascular disease, and overall poor health. My grandfather used to tell me: "I just eat to live and not live to eat. Always eat to live well." Good advice!

After my diabetes wake-up call, I determined to change the way I managed *me*. Through some serious effort, I disciplined myself to eradicate my diabetic condition by diet and exercise. As a result, I lost seventy pounds, and my body fat percentage dropped from 30 percent to 14 percent. My body mass index dropped from well over 30 to 19.5. The commitment paid off. During my most recent physical exam, the doctor confirmed that I was diabetes-free.

Exercise and diet are the keys to managing your body. Why is this so important? In 1 Corinthians 6:19–20, Paul said, "Do you not know that your bodies are temples of the Holy Spirit, who is in you, whom you have received from God? You are not your own; you were bought at a price. Therefore honor God with your bodies." We were designed to manage our bodies according to our divine design.

SPIRITUAL HEALTH

How you manage your spiritual life is important because it connects to your divine design. You were created to have a vibrant relationship with God. Much like your physical health, spiritual health requires daily attention. We are bombarded with all sorts of messages and demands every day, and unless we pause to focus on our spiritual lives, the urgency of life will render our spiritual lives powerless.

According to Jim Rohn, there are eight characteristics of any healthy relationship:

1. Love

2. Serving heart

3. Honest communication

4. Friendliness

5. Patience

6. Loyalty

7. Common purpose

8. Fun[1]

When it comes to your relationship with God, these eight characteristics should be present.

There should be an abiding, consistent *love* for God and respect for His Word. As a result of your love for Him, you should want to *serve* Him. You *communicate* with God by talking to Him in prayer and listening to Him through His Word, sermons, teachers, music, and so forth.

Friendliness suggests an open relationship in which there is nothing to hide. You will be friendly with God when your

---

1   Jim Rohn, "8 Traits of Healthy Relationships," posted at http://www. success.com/article/8-traits-of-healthy-relationships.

motives align with His and your desire is to honor Him in all that you do.

Patience means yielding to the other party. God doesn't move at our pace. We must be patient when we ask

> **We are bombarded with all sorts of messages and demands every day, and unless we pause to focus on our spiritual lives, the urgency of life will render our spiritual lives powerless.**

God for something because what we want might not be the best for us. We can't see our lives from His perspective, so we often grow impatient with His failure to respond.

There is a need for *loyalty* whenever you encounter a situation in which you are torn between honoring God and pursuing what the world has to offer. Your loyalty should always be to God.

We share a *common purpose* with God when we align our lives with His plan. God will never compromise His plan in order to win us to His side.

Fun is a byproduct of the other seven characteristics. When we align our lives with God's plan, our lives will be fun!

You can't maintain good spiritual health without making it a priority. Going to church weekly is a good idea, but it isn't enough to sustain you any more than exercising once a week will keep you in shape. Consider adding these disciplines to your everyday life: Bible reading and study, prayer, conversations with other believers, and encouraging music. Good spiritual health is your responsibility; your church exists "to equip his people for works of service, so that the body of Christ may be built up" (Ephesians 4:12).

EMOTIONAL HEALTH

Emotions are one of the most difficult things to control. Managing them is, therefore, one of the most important tasks for a leader. Everyone has trigger events that stir emotions. Some people are bothered by the way other people drive or by the speed at which the checkout lines flow. Some respond harshly to a specific person or situation. The bottom line is that emotions can take a toll on your overall health.

> **When you replace emotional outbursts with calm responses, you'll feel better about yourself.**

You probably know things that trigger your emotions. Though you can't stop the stimulus, you can alter your response. Emotions have a lot of power. Some people are emotional eaters. Others are emotional spenders. Some people take vacations they can't afford in order to escape situations they can no longer cope with. Gaining control over your emotions might be one of the biggest money-saving strategies around.

Part of military training is to prepare for the "what if" moments. What if the ship starts sinking? What if the aircraft loses power? What if your unit is attacked from behind? We all need similar strategies related to things that can set off an emotional outburst.

Take a few moments, and write down three to five things that routinely fire up your emotions. Then write down a more positive response to each of those situations. Once you have noted your responses, start practicing for the next opportunity. When you replace emotional outbursts with calm responses, you'll feel better about yourself.

DEALING WITH DISAPPOINTMENT

Disappointment is the distance between our expectations and reality. When we expect something amazing to happen and it doesn't happen, we are disappointed. We can't control reality, so we must manage disappointment by managing our expectations. In situations that have the potential to produce disappointment, it is wise to identify a best-case and worst-case scenario up front. If you can deal with the worst-case scenario, then you can prepare in advance to manage your disappointment.

You can also limit disappointment by clearly defining reality. As a leader, defining reality is vital because you don't want to guide your team by making empty promises or overstating the truth. Be honest about the situation with yourself and those you lead. Make sure your communication is clear and that you aren't setting others up to experience disappointment.

AVOIDING TEMPTATION

In 1 Corinthians 10:13, Paul said, "No temptation has overtaken you except what is common to mankind. And God is faithful; he will not let you be tempted beyond what you can bear. But when you are tempted, he will also provide a way out so that you can endure it." In other words, your temptations aren't unique to you.

Why, then, do things that might have negative consequences distract so many people? They simply don't have a plan to avoid temptation. Let's say your weakness is cupcakes. You probably know the dangers associated with going into one of the nearby cupcake stores. This was a problem for me. I had a favorite cupcake store in Kirkland, Washington, called Sweet Cakes. Their red velvet cupcakes were to die for. I had developed a habit of stopping at this place every day, and I knew I had to discipline myself to break this habit. Otherwise, I would pay for it with my physical health.

What happens when your temptation is gossip, wasting time, social media, or something else on the Internet? These temptations are much harder to manage, but the good news is that we have the God-given ability to defend ourselves against any and all temptations. Paul wrote that God "will not let you be tempted beyond what you can bear." You are not a victim.

Stopping to think will eliminate some of the impulsive behaviors that often have catastrophic results. You can avoid a lot of heartache and explaining to your loved ones if you will employ this simple, three-step process when making a decision about giving in to a temptation:

1. **What are the immediate benefits or consequences of this action?** These can be positive or negative. They often are positive because we are very fond of immediate self-gratification.

2. **What are the long-term benefits or consequences of this action?** What will

your life look like if this action becomes a habit? How will you explain this situation to your loved ones and those you lead? These are important considerations that often are discussed only in retrospect.

3. **What are the eternal benefits or consequences of this action?** Eventually, we all will give an account to God for how we invested our lives. He will have one simple, but very probing, question to ask: Why? When temptations come—and they will—our responses will ripple throughout eternity. How many former leaders do you know who never recovered from a moral failure? How many athletes made mistakes that robbed them of their best years?

Your divine design includes the ability to rely on God's power to resist temptations that come your way. You know where your temptations come from. You can usually even predict when they will arrive. Real leaders know how to prepare and defend themselves, so they don't squander the opportunity entrusted to them.

Leadership is about guiding, encouraging, and setting direction for others. But before you can lead others, you must be disciplined in leading yourself. This isn't a matter of simply knowing what to do. Daniel Goleman, author of *Emotional Intelligence,* says that two-thirds of intelligence is emotional;

only one-third is intellectual.[2] You are smarter and make wiser decisions when your emotions are under control. Few emotional decisions are the right decisions.

MANAGING YOURSELF

Self-management requires courage, self-control, and confidence—the building blocks for integrity, conscientiousness, and trustworthiness. These characteristics make others want to follow you. When you have integrity, followers will forgive your mistakes and look for ways to contribute to the overall success of the team. In short, the character of the leader is contagious. You'll attract people who are like you, and you'll see those who aren't like you leave for other opportunities. If good people are coming and marginal ones are going, you've got things moving in the right direction. However, if the good people are leaving and you're left with those who concern you, you might want to take a closer look at how you are managing yourself.

James 1:19–21 says:

> My dear brothers and sisters, take note of this: Everyone should be quick to listen, slow to speak and slow to become angry, because human anger does not produce the righteousness that God desires. Therefore, get rid of all moral filth and the evil that is so prevalent and humbly accept the word planted in you, which can save you.

---

2   Daniel Goleman, *Emotional Intelligence: Why It Can Matter More Than IQ* (New York: Bantam Books, 2005).

James connected a person's emotions to his or her morality. The battle between the sinful nature and the new nature is ongoing. People are watching to see how you and I respond to this battle. That's why it is so vital that we monitor the emotional signs we send.

A mentor of mine, Don Argue, repeatedly told me, "You have to be careful what you say because you are the leader." People cling to the words of their leaders. They trust their leaders until the leaders prove they can't be trusted. They expect their leaders to demonstrate a level of self-management that inspires them to do the same.

> The character of the leader is contagious.

It's not easy to manage *me*. I push back against my own commitments all the time. Although I don't always want to, I am at the gym every morning at six o'clock. I know exercise releases endorphins that awaken me to a higher level of intensity and productivity. I allow time for personal reflection because calming my soul helps me prepare for the day mentally and emotionally. I also build into my schedule time for relationships because they sharpen me and make me wiser.

"As iron sharpens iron, so one person sharpens another" (Proverbs 27:17). We need people in our lives to make us stronger. We also need to recognize our unique divine designs. We will be better leaders when we make leading ourselves a priority.

KEY IDEAS

- We have been entrusted with amazing resources that should be used in accordance with the wishes of the One who entrusted them to us.

- View food as fuel for the life you want to live. Good fuel produces a healthy life; bad fuel leads to a number of problems.

- You were created to have a vibrant relationship with God. Much like physical health, your spiritual health requires daily attention.

- Disappointment is the distance between our expectations and reality.

- Before you can lead others, you must be disciplined in leading yourself.

DISCUSSION QUESTIONS

1. List some of the resources God has entrusted to you. How do you know what God wants you to do with all He has entrusted to you?

2. Reflect on the food you consumed in the last twenty-four hours. Does your diet fuel the kind of life you want to have? Explain your response.

3. What is your strategy for strengthening your spiritual life?

4. How have you handled disappointment? What have you learned about yourself as a result of your disappointments?

5. "Before you can lead others, you must be disciplined in leading yourself." How do you lead yourself, and who holds you accountable?

YOUR NEXT STEPS

1. Review all of the areas of self-management discussed in this chapter, and look for ways to manage yourself better. Establish some criteria for evaluating your progress.

2. Make a food and exercise journal, or use an online tool to track your food and exercise for the next few weeks. Note how you feel each day and your productivity.

3. Identify two or three books you can read that will motivate you to manage yourself more effectively. (See the Recommended Reading list in appendix 3.)

THE DISCIPLINE OF
SELF-PREPAREDNESS

"THE WILL TO SUCCEED IS IMPORTANT,
BUT WHAT'S MORE IMPORTANT IS THE
WILL TO PREPARE."

—BOBBY KNIGHT

How many opportunities do you have in a day? Fifty? A few hundred? Thousands? The truth is you don't really know how many opportunities you have unless you take action. Situations that aren't acted upon aren't opportunities.

If we aren't preparing ourselves, we are growing complacent. There is no neutral ground. God always keeps shaping us, so we must be ready to accept new opportunities even when we are comfortable in the existing situation. We all learn this lesson sooner or later.

Have you ever noticed how many players on a football team never get into a game? Professional teams have at least two backup quarterbacks who practice each week and learn the opposition's defensive schemes. They throw passes, call audibles, and run the offense while knowing their chances of playing on

Sunday are slim. So why do they go through the preparation? They do it because it's their job. If something happens to the starting quarterback, they must be ready to put down the clipboard and pick up the mouthpiece. Several star players got their breaks when they stepped in to replace an injured player, and if they hadn't been prepared, they might have missed their golden opportunity.

> No matter where you are in life or in an organization, be excellent at what you do.

Backup quarterbacks prepare to play while knowing they might never get in the game. They workout and learn. They try to improve their skills. They know opportunity doesn't have a pause button, so they must be ready.

Leaders are no different. You might be reading this while dreaming about the day you will be a leader. Or you might already be one but have lost your drive for excellence. Consider this your pep talk!

Some people go through life willing to accept "good enough" as their standard of excellence. Those people will never become leaders of influence. No matter where you are in life or in an organization, be excellent at what you do. Peter said it this way:

> Each of you should use whatever gift you have received to serve others, as faithful stewards of God's grace in its various forms. If anyone speaks, they should do so as one who speaks the very words of God. If anyone serves, they should do so with the strength

God provides, so that in all things God may be praised through Jesus Christ (1 Peter 4:10–11).

Whatever you do, do it as if you are doing it for God. That standard can change a lot about the way leaders do things. You might have been one of those college students who asked your professors how much work you needed to do to earn a C in the class. You might have been an employee who did the minimum required to earn your paycheck. If that has been your attitude and you are now in a position of leadership, you have successfully defied the odds. Most people who accept mediocre living never make it to the leadership ranks.

Dynamic leaders always look for ways to improve their skills. They never stop developing. Abraham became a world traveler at age seventy. Moses learned a new skill set at forty. Susan Boyle was the surprising winner of *Britain's Got Talent* at age forty-eight. Laura Ingalls Wilder wrote the first book on which the television show *Little House on the Prairie* was based when she was sixty-four. At age seventy-six, Nelson Mandela was elected president of South Africa. Julia Child started her television show, *The French Chef,* when she was fifty-one. Peter Mark Roget published his thesaurus at age seventy-three.[3] All of these people were committed to the task long before they experienced success.

If you aren't growing, you are going backwards. The world is changing at a breakneck pace, and anyone who doesn't keep

---

3   Molly Edmonds and Becky Striepe, "10 Famous Accomplishments made Late in Life," posted at http://health.howstuffworks.com/wellness/aging/senior-health-lifestyle/5-famous-accomplishments-made-late-in-life.htm#page=0.

up will quickly become irrelevant. This requires a commitment to lifelong learning and growing.

WHY DO LEADERS STOP GROWING?

If you study the stories of leaders who have sustained success over a long period of time, you'll find some attitudes that they did *not* have. Leaders who fizzle, however, often demonstrate one or more of the following characteristics:

1. **They think they have arrived.** Some leaders experience a small degree of success and believe they have reached their pinnacle. They rest on their laurels and eventually become as relevant as the video rental store. Has anyone seen one of those lately?

2. **They rely on what they did in the past.** It's surprising how many leaders try to guide their teams into the future by relying on what worked decades ago. Doing what you've always done won't produce results you haven't yet experienced. Leaders who rely on past strategies have already seen their best days. If you're still using overhead projectors and flannel boards, it's time to move into this century!

3. **They serve a position, not a constituency.** The Peter Principle states that people will be promoted until they reach their level of

incompetence.[4] When this happens, leaders rely on their titles rather than their skills to guide their teams. Leaders should be selected based on their effectiveness and influence because an organization will never outperform its leaders. If you have inefficient and ineffective leaders, you'll have an organization that squanders its resources and eventually fails.

4. **They think the organization exists to serve them.** Unethical leaders often view their organizations as a means to an end. They misuse resources for their own good. They take advantage of the flexibility built into the schedule. They use their platforms to elicit personal favors. Eventually, they find themselves explaining their actions to a board or a government agency. Leaders who are always looking for what's in it for themselves will never guide an organization toward its best days.

The world today is a different place than even a few years ago. The next generation values technology, immediacy, and community. They've grown up in a digital environment and expect those who lead them to have a penchant for the things they think are important. They want to know that what they are doing has value. The iGeneration comes to school carrying mobile devices and posting to social media everything that happens—

---

4   "Peter Principle," posted at http://en.wikipedia.org/wiki/Peter_Principle

good and bad. Your reputation as a leader and your organization's reputation are being built 140 characters at a time.

Professors must constantly learn new theories and developments in their areas of expertise. If they don't stay on the cutting edge, they won't be able to prepare students for success in their chosen fields. School administrators must learn how to leverage online learning, MOOCs (Massive Open Online Courses), and customizable curriculum plans if their schools are to attract the new generation of learners.

> **People and organizations that don't adapt will become irrelevant.**

Church leaders must carefully evaluate the effectiveness of their traditions and how they affect the interest of younger adults. Far too many church leaders are more concerned with protecting traditions than providing value to their congregations and communities. There is more than one way to share the message of the gospel. We can alter methodologies without compromising our theology. The truth never changes, but how we present truth must maintain a social relevance.

People and organizations that don't adapt will become irrelevant. The sigmoid curve, or S-curve, represents the lifecycle of almost every business or organization. Your organization or team must monitor itself and adjust according to these four lifecycle phases in order to succeed over a long period of time:

1. **Inception.** This is when things are starting out. Resources are invested without significant return because people simply don't know about

your organization or product. From a business perspective, there is a slight dip.

2. **Growth.** Things pick up after the word gets out and people begin to recognize their need for your product or service. This is when you begin to experience dividends from your investment. People start coming to your church, buying your products, or enlisting your services. The business turns upward, and growth is rapid and significant.

3. **Maturity.** After a while, things begin to level off. Maybe your product has loyal customers, but many have turned to the next big thing. Your consulting firm's affinity for historical strategies might have been overshadowed by new strategies coming from more relevant firms. Your church might go into maintenance mode where the number of new people coming balances the number of people who are leaving. The bottom line flattens, and things stagnate. This is when many leaders panic and look for quick fixes.

4. **Decline.** The fourth stage is the downward slide as things begin to fade. This stage is fatal to some organizations. People talk about "success" in the past tense and begin to leave the organization. Businesses find themselves in the red because the cost of doing business exceeds revenue.

The S-curve doesn't have to be fatal; it can be used to grow and sustain your business or organization. All you need to do is monitor your position on the curve. The best time to plan your next big thing isn't when the current thing expires but in the midst of your most successful times. Starting anything new produces tension, but it helps sharpen your focus and propel your team, business, or organization to even greater success.

As a leader, you must be prepared for the S-curve. You need to know where you are on the curve and continually work toward launching whatever is next *before* you reach maturity and decline. The greatest obstacle to success is the lack of preparedness. Leaders who are prepared will guide their teams efficiently, create vibrant environments, and cultivate the respect of others.

If you let Him, God will always be shaping you for what's next. You might remember the parable of the talents in Matthew 25:14–30. Jesus told the story about a man who went on a journey and entrusted his wealth to three servants. Some translations of the Bible use the term "talent" to describe the amount of money. A talent was worth several thousand *denarii*. A denarius was a day's wage for a servant. Therefore, a talent was the same as twenty years of wages, and today, a talent would be worth more than $300,000.

The three servants represent two different responses. The first two servants invested their resources and earned a return. The third servant hid what he had been given. To put it into simple language: the first two did something while the third did nothing.

We don't know what took place in the lives of the servants before they were given the money. We do know, however, that two of them were prepared to do the right thing and the third one was not. As leaders, we must constantly prepare ourselves for whatever is coming even though we don't know what it is.

The future always favors those who are prepared. George Washington Carver said, "There is no shortcut to achievement. Life requires thorough preparation—veneer isn't worth anything."

I appreciate the story about a young man who once approached a logging crew foreman to ask for a job. "Let's see you chop down this tree," replied the foreman. The young man stepped forward and took down a large tree. The foreman was impressed and said, "You can start Monday."

The young man reported to work faithfully each day, but on Thursday afternoon the foreman went to the young man and said, "You can pick up your pay check on the way out today."

The young man was surprised and asked, "Don't we get paid on Friday?"

"Yes we do," the foreman replied. "But I'm letting you go because you've fallen behind. Our productivity charts show that you have dropped from first place on Monday to last place today." "I'm the hardest worker here," the young man objected. "I arrive first, leave last, and even have worked through my breaks!"

The foreman could see young man's sincerity. He hesitated for a moment and asked, "Have you been sharpening your axe?"

The young man stood quietly and said, "No sir, I've been working too hard to take time for that!"

As a leader, you must take time to sharpen your axe. Don't get so busy that you lose sight of what it means to be a leader. Prepare yourself to lead by tapping into your divine design. Those who sharpen their axes will outperform those who don't.

KEY IDEAS

- You don't really know how many opportunities you have unless you take action because situations that aren't acted upon aren't opportunities.

- No matter where you are in life or in an organization, be excellent at what you do.

- Doing what you've always done won't produce results you haven't yet experienced.

- People and organizations that don't adapt will die.

- The best time to plan your next big thing isn't when the current thing expires but in the midst of your most successful times.

DISCUSSION QUESTIONS

1. Think of some situations that never developed into opportunities. Why did you choose not to take action?

2. What are some examples of things you do to be excellent? How does your pursuit of excellence affect those around you?

3. What are three things you can do to pursue improved results in your areas of responsibility? What is your plan for taking action?

4. Look back over the past several years. In what ways have you adapted? How will your willingness to adapt affect the next few years?

5. What successes are you experiencing right now? How can you leverage your success to keep moving forward in life?

YOUR NEXT STEPS

1. Take time to reflect on your present situation. Identify some opportunities that might be on the horizon.

2. Create a checklist you can use to evaluate your leadership environments. Use the checklist to identify areas in which you need to improve.

3. Identify a class or conference you can attend that will help you "sharpen your axe."

THE DISCIPLINE OF
CHARACTER

"BE MORE CONCERNED WITH YOUR
CHARACTER THAN YOUR REPUTATION,
BECAUSE YOUR CHARACTER IS WHAT YOU
REALLY ARE, WHILE YOUR REPUTATION IS
MERELY WHAT OTHERS THINK YOU ARE."
—*JOHN WOODEN*

The dictionary defines *character* as "the aggregate of features and traits that form the individual nature of some person or thing; moral or ethical quality; qualities of honesty, courage, or the like; integrity: reputation; good repute; an account of the qualities or peculiarities of a person or thing."[5] Character is one of those traits you don't really think about unless it's missing. It's easy to overlook character in leaders because *it is expected,* but when leaders lack character, it shows.

Bad character kills the potential for influence whereas strong character creates opportunities for influence. We've all

5   Dictionary.com, "character," posted at http://dictionary.reference.com/browse/character?s=t

seen the stories about political or religious leaders who had moral failures. These stories make the news because people expect leaders to have impeccable character. Leaders don't have to be perfect—we all make mistakes—but there should be an underlying foundation of integrity that governs a leader's thoughts and actions. Leaders who lack integrity won't be leaders very long.

Bad character always keeps people from maximizing their potential. Far too many leaders have squandered opportunities to become exceptional leaders because they lacked the discipline of character. They had opportunities but didn't have the character necessary to step into those opportunities. They had talent, but talent without character never produces leaders. They had desire, but their inability to live with integrity redirected their vision and left them with nothing but empty promises and unfulfilled dreams.

> **You can be a highly effective leader if you'll cultivate the discipline of character.**

It doesn't have to be that way. You can be a highly effective leader if you'll cultivate the discipline of character. Our campus pastor, Andrew Gard, and his wife, Christina, created a discipleship tool that includes the *Life Journal* for our community at Southeastern University. We use it with more than twelve hundred students in our Connect Groups, our university-wide mentoring program.

The program focuses on four basic disciplines: devotion, service, reflection, and focus. Through this program, we create environments where character-based relationships are developed and nurtured. Our faculty, staff, and administrators meet one-on-one with students for ten consecutive weeks in small groups. They offer wisdom and experience to help students grow in their faith and succeed in their careers. In these relational environments, character becomes a necessary ingredient and a desired byproduct.

Although character is contagious, it also must be taught. But our culture is not a believable teacher of character. We live in a world where character is often ridiculed. Young people sometimes sacrifice social acceptance by making a moral purity pledge. Politicians who stand up for biblical values often find their character attacked by opponents. Athletes who refuse to embrace the self-indulgent lifestyle popularized by television and the media can become the brunt of jokes. We live in a character vacuum.

Character, however, is part of the fabric of quality leaders. Character encompasses who you are, how you are developing, and who you are becoming. How you do life demonstrates your character.

WHO ARE YOU?

Who are you, *really?* That's a better question, because it forces you to set aside your image and focus on reality.

Who are you when no one is looking? Is the character people see in everyday life the same one that surfs the Internet in your office or completes tax forms every spring? Character permeates every aspect of life, and the lack of character shows, too. If we cultivate attitudes that align with our divine design and continually do the right things even when no one is watching, eventually our character will be reflected in those we lead.

No matter who you claim to be, the truth eventually will be known. Dishonesty in one area of life will lead to dishonesty in other areas. Most moral crises start as a subtle shift from the biblical standard. No one sets out to embezzle millions of dollars; it might have started just by falsifying travel reimbursement requests.

HOW ARE YOU DEVELOPING?

You eventually reflect the influences you allow into your life. You will become like your five closest friends. You'll exhibit the attitudes of the books you read and the music you listen to. The old computer adage says, "Garbage in, garbage out," And our lives are much the same.

Although the computer saying is dated, it is accurate. Computers can't turn bad input into good output. You can't either. Take a close look at the things you think about, talk about, and dream about. Are those things rooted in integrity or in something else? The more you evaluate experiences, the better you'll be able to identify what you allow to influence your development.

WHO ARE YOU BECOMING?

The S-curve we discussed in the previous chapter can be used to describe a variety of situations. You can plot your personal progress on the curve and anticipate where you are headed. As a leader, you can be in any of the four stages—inception, growth, maturity, or decline.

When you start out in leadership or in a new leadership position, you are in the inception stage. That's the time when you work hard to establish yourself as a leader and earn the respect of others. The amount of work you do might have limited effects, but don't worry, the next stage will more than make up for it.

A leader in the growth stage experiences great success. Things go well—some even call this the honeymoon phase. All of the hard work during the inception stage starts paying off. Your influence grows, and people respond positively to your initiatives. Most leaders remember these days for a long time.

The next step on the S-curve is the maturity stage. In leadership, this can also be called the "uh-oh stage." Growth fizzles, and successes become sporadic. If there are any critics, they step up and begin expressing concerns. Some of them will be louder than others. When this happens, leaders have a choice of pressing on and starting something new (inception again), continuing what they've been doing and move into decline, or focusing on the past by resurrecting traditions and celebrating what used to be (stagnation). The unfortunate truth is that leaders who let things get to this stage will have a hard time recapturing the excitement that characterized the growth stage.

The final stage is decline. Leadership influence fades, and the leader experiences pressure to right the ship or be replaced. Shareholders in the organization grow weary of relying on the past and challenge the leader to get things moving again. This stage can be characterized by heightened tension and anxiety on the part of everyone involved. Leaders in decline are sometimes forced to resign.

Forced termination is never easy. It's not easy for the organization, its supervisory team, or the leader. When leaders are forced out, the teams they led suffer. No one wins when this happens. The only way to prevent this is by carefully evaluating where you are in the S-curve. You might find it helpful to create a small group of people who will help you honestly evaluate your progress as a leader and your organization's progress with respect to its agreed-upon goals.

THE DARK SIDE OF LEADERSHIP

Every leader must learn how to deal with the moral compass in his or her life. Moral failure probably claims more leaders than any other threat. Why do leaders fail morally? Every leader in the Bible faced life-altering temptations. Some allowed their moral compasses to guide them to safety while others ignored their compasses and gave in to the desire for self-gratification.

Self-gratification is one of the greatest threats facing leaders. Your journey to a leadership position might be very unique, like mine. It could be that your journey into leadership was the logical progression for someone in your field or your company. Regardless of how you got there, you might be tempted to sit back on your laurels and take in the scenery. After all, you worked hard. You proved your leadership capability. You probably sat through countless boring meetings and acted interested.

Once you settle into your leadership role, you are likely to discover some perks that come with the territory. Depending upon your position, perks can range from small things like a printer in your office to big things like twenty-four-hour access to a corporate jet. It's easy to start thinking about what you *deserve*, and that's when danger comes knocking.

Second Samuel 11 tells the story of David's moral failure. David had been anointed king of Israel when he was a teenage shepherd. He eventually killed **Moral failure probably claims more leaders than any other threat.** Goliath while on a trip to take supplies to his older brothers and was celebrated for his heroism. However, David had a dark side. He faked being insane to avoid danger, and he grew more arrogant as his successes were celebrated.

Usually, kings accompanied their men to the battlefield, but in 2 Samuel 11, David sent his men to battle while he stayed home. In avoiding his responsibility, he set the stage for a tragic course of events. David saw a beautiful woman bathing and ordered that she be brought to him. He ignored the fact that the woman was married and took advantage of his power as the king. She became pregnant, and David tried to cover it up. When his plan failed, he ordered her husband to the front lines so he would die in battle. His adultery, deception, and murder were just the beginning. In 2 Samuel 12:11–12, God said to David through the prophet Nathan:

> This is what the LORD says: "Out of your own household I am going to bring calamity on you. Before your very eyes I will take your wives and give them to one who is close to you, and he will sleep with your

wives in broad daylight. You did it in secret, but I will
do this thing in broad daylight before all Israel."

What happened to David? The man who was so close to God lost sight of his moral compass. He made decisions based on what he wanted rather than on what God said. His choices were tragic, and such choices will be tragic for you as well.

Earlier, we talked about the power of temptation. You know where temptation originates for you. You know the things that can derail and distract you, so protect yourself against them. Put in place standards that you refuse to violate. If you are married, for instance, never be alone with a member of the opposite sex. Don't ride in the car, have dinner, or stop by a coffee shop without a third party present. Protect your reputation by installing an Internet filter that prevents you or anyone else from accessing inappropriate content. Even if you think you deleted a file or something from your history, it is still there and can be discovered.

> I would prefer to follow someone who deserves to be followed but doesn't demand it than to be required to follow someone who demands it.

Be careful how you use social media. Don't say anything to anyone that you don't want to become public knowledge. Because of your position, people will repeat what you say. Even things said in jest can become sources of trouble. Determine your moral boundaries, and put guardrails in place to protect yourself from crossing them. Explain the boundaries to your spouse and support staff. Enlist those who work with you to help protect your reputation and influence.

When I first arrived at Southeastern University, Chris Owen, Vice-President of Student Development, asked me what I dislike the most. "Arrogance," I said. Arrogance prevented the Pharisees from accepting Jesus Christ as the Messiah, and arrogance in our lives makes us think we are above the law or beyond reproach. Arrogance is present in today's church as leaders manipulate people and data to earn accolades that land them on some "Top Ten" list.

Jesus addressed the problem of arrogance in the Sermon on the Mount (Matthew 5–7). He began with a statement of the Beatitudes, character traits that should be foundational for every believer. The characteristics should be required for anyone who wants to be a leader. Jesus encouraged humility, compassion, generosity, mercy, purity, spiritual hunger, and a passion for peace. Taking on these traits doesn't weaken leaders, it makes them stronger and more effective.

I would prefer to follow someone who deserves to be followed but doesn't demand it than to be required to follow someone who demands it. Jerk leaders lead jerk organizations! Great leaders can lead and leave an organization, and the organization remains healthy. No enduring leader ever leaves an organization and watches it collapse. When that happens, the leader is really saying, "It was all about me."

DEVELOPING CHARACTER

As I said at the beginning of this chapter, people expect good character from their leaders, so it's a foregone conclusion that character matters. In your leadership role, you should work hard to exhibit character because your organization will eventually reflect who you are. So what can you do to develop character? Here are some suggestions:

1. **Do what you say you will do, even when it's difficult.**

2. **If there's something you wouldn't be willing to do yourself, don't delegate it.**

3. **Take responsibility for your decisions.** Don't look for ways to blame others. Be a leader by owning what you decide. If you don't want to own it, don't choose to do it.

4. **Be able to explain your rationale for doing what you do.** You might not have to explain it, but you should be prepared to, just in case someone asks.

5. **Know your boundaries and the boundaries of others.** Don't let your position of leadership make you oblivious to the boundaries of those you lead. Show respect, and you'll earn respect.

6. **Cultivate self-discipline, but don't use your self-discipline as a weapon against people you lead.** Lead by example, not by proclamation.

7. **Understand your strengths, and don't apologize for working within them.** At the same time, don't be afraid to delegate those things that are not within your strengths. When you ask someone to do something you know you can't or shouldn't do, publicly praise and thank him or her.

8. **Know when to turn off the lights and go home.** Your job shouldn't be your life. Encourage those you lead to spend time with their families by making time with your family a priority.

9. **Learn to distinguish between your needs and your wants.** Don't confuse the two or use your position of authority to treat your wants like needs.

10. **Tell the truth all the time.** If you always tell the truth, you'll never have to remember what you told different people. If you expect others to be truthful, be truthful with them. That doesn't mean telling everything you know. Use discretion when sharing information that doesn't need to be broadcast.

It all comes down to who you *are,* not what you *do.* When you have character, you will earn the respect and admiration of those you lead. Colin Powell said:

Leadership is solving problems. The day soldiers stop bringing you their problems is the day you have stopped leading them. They have either lost confidence that you can help or concluded you do not care. Either case is a failure of leadership.[6]

No matter what you do as a leader, your reputation will outlive your position. I don't know all the stories of the people I've had the privilege of leading, but I do know that some of today's sharpest young minds are products of the university I lead. I can't take credit for their academic accomplishments— that belongs to the dedication of the students and faculty—but I am responsible for the environment in which their education takes place. As the leader, I set the tone. When I interact with trustees or students, my character shows. I must take who I am seriously, because the task I've been given to do is overwhelming.

I'm not in my position of leadership because I'm good; I'm here because God is good. He has a divine design for me. He has a divine design for you, too. May we humble ourselves before Him as we step into the roles He has for us.

---

6   Oren Harai, *The Leadership Secrets of Colin Powell* (New York: McGraw-Hill, 2003), 36.

KEY IDEAS

- Bad character kills the potential for influence whereas strong character creates opportunities for influence.

- No matter who you claim to be, the truth eventually will be known. Dishonesty in one area of life will lead to dishonesty in other areas.

- Self-gratification is one of the greatest threats facing leaders.

- In your leadership role, you should work hard to exhibit character because your organization will eventually reflect who you are.

- No matter what you do as a leader, your reputation will outlive your position.

DISCUSSION QUESTIONS

1. What are some practical ways you can develop and protect your character?

2. Give an example of a time when you had to give someone some unpleasant news. How did you decide what to say?

3. Who in your life helps keep you grounded so you don't succumb to the temptation to seek self-gratification?

4. Reflect on your organization. In what ways does it exhibit your character? Are there elements of your character that you don't want your organization to exhibit?

5. How has the reputation and work of your predecessors affected your ability to do your job? What should you do to set up for success the leader who will follow you?

YOUR NEXT STEPS

1. Make a list of character traits you admire and those you despise. Complete a self-evaluation, identifying strengths you can use and weaknesses that need correction.

2. Ask a trusted advisor or friend to hold you accountable for the development of your character. Commit to complete honesty and confidentiality in all discussions.

3. Write down a description of the organization you want to leave to the leader who will follow you. Create some action points to guide your progress toward these goals.

THE DISCIPLINE OF
RELATIONSHIPS

"THE MORE THAT YOU READ,
THE MORE THINGS YOU WILL KNOW.
THE MORE THAT YOU LEARN,
THE MORE PLACES YOU'LL GO."
—*DR. SEUSS*

No matter what your station in life, relationships are part of it. From the deepest interpersonal relationships with your spouse and immediate family to the passing relationships you have with the barista or neighbor, relationships are woven into every part of life.

You can't fulfill your divine design without relationships. You were created for relationships. God's plan for your life includes relational intimacy with Him as well as with others. There's no escaping it. I can look back and see how God used different people to change me and shape me. I also can look around and see people God is using to influence me today. There is no doubt in my mind that I wouldn't be where I am today without the encouraging people God placed in my life.

I'll never forget Pastor Fred Cottriel. He was my pastor at Bakersfield First Assembly in Bakersfield, California, when I was a teenager. Pastor Cottriel was a true *investing* pastor, a servant mentor. One Sunday morning after a church service, he told me that he had been observing my life. He believed I had gifts, talent, and abilities God had placed in my life for future ministry leadership, and he wanted to invest the time to mentor me. So, at the age of fifteen, I began spending one day a week with Pastor Cottriel. He took me on hospital visitations, newcomer visits, and he even taught me how he crafted his weekly sermons.

Years later, when God opened the doors of ministry to me, what Pastor Cottriel had poured into my life made a huge difference in my ability to handle the call. I still benefit from what he gave me through our relationship. Pastor Cottriel emphasized over and over again that God designed each of us with intentional purpose. We were created to hit the missional bull's-eye of His intended target.

In our technologically-connected society, people too easily lose sight of the importance of high quality relationships. It's hard for them to distinguish between social media followers or friends and real people. That's why people can be well-connected yet lonely.

Steve Saccone, author of *Relational Intelligence,* said, "The substance of your conversations mirrors the substance of the relationships you have in your life."[7] As leaders, we set the tone in our dialogues and relationships. This is a different way of thinking for some people because they see themselves as the

---

7   Steve Saccone, from the video "What Our Words Reveal About Us," posted at https://www.youtube.com/watch?v=2uqycvV_iUE.

object of their relationships. They abdicate their positions of power and authority when interacting with certain people.

Leaders have the responsibility to establish their leadership relationships. It is the job of leaders to learn about the people they lead, so they can empower them to embrace their divine designs. You can't know the potential of an organization until you know its people, and you don't get to know people by staying aloof and disconnected. You must be willing to step into their worlds and learn from them without stepping out of your role as a leader. There is a delicate balance between the two, but it can be done if you pay attention to the key components of healthy relationships.

> **It is the job of leaders to learn about the people they lead, so they can empower them to embrace their divine designs.**

EMPOWERMENT

Empowerment is the act of giving power or authority to someone to do what he or she is qualified and motivated to do. How many times do we invite people into our organizations and assign them tasks without understanding how they are wired and what their divine designs really are? This is a disservice to the organization and to the people.

I've seen church leaders do this repeatedly and then wonder why new people never started serving or decided to leave the church. They totally miss the point of empowerment. In Ephesians 4:11–13, Paul wrote:

So Christ himself gave the apostles, the prophets, the evangelists, the pastors and teachers, to equip his people for works of service, so that the body of Christ may be built up until we all reach unity in the faith and in the knowledge of the Son of God and become mature, attaining to the whole measure of the fullness of Christ.

Look closely at Paul's words. God gave church leaders the responsibility of equipping His people to live out their divine designs. This statement probably sends shock waves through the minds of many church leaders. They've never thought much about their equipping and empowering responsibilities. Their strategy has been simple but ineffective: "We have a need for nursery workers, and you are a new member. God obviously brought you here to meet our need." Most church leaders never say it that way, to be sure, but it works out that way in the end.

The process of empowerment takes on an entrepreneurial flair. God might bring new people to your church or organization to help you do things you aren't currently doing, but plugging people into holes on an organizational chart is not equipping them for works of service.

You can't empower someone you don't know. Therefore, you must be willing to invest in relationships, so you can learn how to empower others. As you get to know people, you will discover their passions and desires. That's when you can make a call regarding the type of empowerment to be offered. You might empower someone to lead a new initiative, or you could offer them an opportunity to work within a strategy that already is in place. Either way, you'll have a clearer understanding about empowerment when you get to know that individual.

What happens when people don't feel empowered? In the church world, people begin to lose their enthusiasm. They move from active to passive, from involved to aware. Eventually, people who aren't empowered will seek opportunities somewhere else. They'll move from church to church, looking for a place that will equip and empower them to fulfill their divine designs.

> **The quality of your relationships is dramatically affected by the degree of trust others have in you.**

In business, the same thing happens. Employees lose their enthusiasm for the company, its products, and purposes. They become clock-watchers and sick-time-takers. They work to get the paycheck but aren't really invested in their jobs. Then they begin looking for a new place to work. They jump from job to job, looking for a place that will empower them to do what they were designed and trained to do.

Relationships are a prerequisite for empowerment. Without strong relationships, it is impossible to lead your team or organization to be the best it can be.

TRUST

Do the people you lead trust you? Albert Einstein said, "Whoever is careless with the truth in small matters cannot be trusted with important matters." The quality of your relationships is dramatically affected by the degree of trust others have in you.

Trust can be eroded in a matter of seconds, and once violated, takes a long time to rebuild.

Here are some practical things you can do to build trust:

1. **Lead by example.** If your actions contradict your words, people will believe what they *see*. If you trust those you lead to do their jobs, they will trust your leadership, and your relationships will be strong.

2. **Communicate clearly.** Many people in leadership seem to have an unfortunate knack for making simple things complicated. I've certainly seen this in the academic world. But why use fourteen-letter words when a much shorter word would do the job better? Clear communication creates a healthy two-way environment. If you communicate clearly, your team will communicate clearly with you.

3. **Get to know each other.** Use one of the self-assessment tools mentioned earlier to create a dialog within your team. The better people know each other, the better the working environment will be.

4. **Don't play the blame game.** Mistakes are going to happen. As the leader, you can earn a lot of trust by shouldering your responsibility and showing mercy. Jack Welch said, "I've learned that mistakes can often be as good a teacher as success." When

there is a mistake, take collective responsibility for it, and process it as a learning experience.

5. **Discuss trust.** The sooner you talk about something, the less destructive it will be. If there is an obvious issue with trust, talk about it, first with the individual and then with any individuals who were affected by it. Praise publicly, but criticize privately.[8]

COLLABORATION AND COOPERATION

The difference between great organizations and mediocre organizations is the people. The church is simply an organization fueled by the collective presence of God in the individuals who are part of it. Organizations are synergistic in that they are more powerful than the sum of their constituent parts. That's why we need to work together. Alexander Graham Bell said:

Great discoveries and improvements invariably involve the cooperation of many minds. I may be given credit for having blazed the trail, but when I look at the subsequent developments I feel the credit is due to others rather than to myself.[9]

---

8   These five points are adapted from "Building Trust Inside Your Team," posted at http://www.mindtools.com/pages/article/building-trust-team. htm.

9   http://www.brainyquote.com/quotes/quotes/a/alexanderg393245.html

As a leader, you might get the credit for the accomplishments of your team or organization. Your ability to acknowledge the contributions of others will go a long way toward deepening the relationships you have with the people who helped make you successful.

A pastor I know had a parking lot conversation with a member of his congregation about an upcoming mission emphasis. The church member shared a few successful strategies she had used in the past and expressed interest in establishing them at his church. She went on to describe her ideas in detail. The following Sunday, the pastor announced a new missions initiative based on his conversation in the parking lot. He never acknowledged that the ideas came from someone else but, instead, took all the credit for ideas he got from her.

In the academic world, we take plagiarism seriously. It can lead to the expulsion of a student. How many times, however, are we guilty of intellectual plagiarism? When we "borrow" ideas and pass them off as our own, we are not only dishonest, but we also harm relationships and discredit ourselves.

It's hard for people to trust leaders they don't really know. I've heard about university presidents who had limited exposure to their students, staff, and faculty, but I take a different approach. I meet personally with the constituency, friends, supporters, staff, faculty, and students at Southeastern University. The culture and perception of SEU has changed because of these relationships. Yet they didn't just happen; it takes a lot of work.

Building relationships has always been part of my strategy. George O. Wood, General Superintendent of the Assemblies of God, USA, once called me about taking the pastoral responsibility at a struggling church in southern California. He offered me the opportunity to lead it back to the vibrancy it once had. Needless to say, the situation was challenging. Although there were about fifteen people attending the church with an average age of seventy, they were in the middle of a younger community—the average age being thirty-five. The church had little money, a five thousand square-foot building in disrepair, and a worship center that would only seat one hundred. To say the least, they were not positioned for success!

So, what was my strategy? I started building relationships. I led the church to do things to engage the community and change its perception of the church. I worked with the limited resources available and guided the congregation to take action. As they got involved in the community, the people of the church began to identify things that needed to be done. One member discovered that people in the neighborhood were saying, "How can this church take care of people if it can't take care of its own property?" That's when people started dreaming again. That's the power of relationships.

All of life is about relationships. Without them, life is empty. Some relationships are taxing and will wear you out, but that's okay. Some people need you more than you need them. As a university president, I understand the value of relationships. Without people, we can't fulfill the mission of the university. Our programs, plans, and facilities are meaningless without students.

As a leader, you must learn how to network, empower, and recognize the value of others. Some people warrant special attention. You should be looking for relationships in which you can invest yourself while allowing others to invest in you.

Every time I begin a mentoring relationship, I discover the principle of reverse mentoring. In other words, I learn a lot from the people I lead. We must maintain a humble posture and not let our positions close the flow of care, concern, and teaching.

I'm reminded of an unfortunate situation in a large, growing church. Its leader takes a top-down approach. The pastor is reluctant to hire someone he fears might outperform him. His personal insecurities keep him from enabling his church to be the best it can be.

I hire people to shore up my weaknesses. I'm a big-picture dreamer, for instance, so I hire detail-oriented people. They need my vision; I need their expertise. It's a healthy relationship based on mutual respect and admiration.

Bill Hackett, Southeastern University Provost, has two decades of academic administrative experience. He is a valuable resource because he freely shares his wisdom and wealth of experience with me. I am a better leader because of our relationship.

Growing relationships is hard. In fact, it's a lot like exercising. You can't grow muscle without tension and pain. If you allow your character to guide you, the relationships you develop will make you a stronger, more trustworthy leader. Isn't that what you want to be?

KEY IDEAS

- In our technologically-connected society, people can easily lose sight of the importance of high quality relationships.

- Empowerment is the act of giving power or authority to someone to do what he or she is qualified and motivated to do.

- Lead by example. If your actions contradict your words, people will believe what they see.

- The difference between great organizations and mediocre organizations is the people.

- If you allow your character to guide you, the relationships you develop will make you a stronger, more trustworthy leader.

DISCUSSION QUESTIONS

1. Describe the characteristics of your strongest relationships. How did those relationships develop, and how do you maintain them?

2. If those you lead were surveyed, what would they say about their feelings of empowerment? To what degree are you satisfied with your empowerment process?

3. What is your greatest leadership skill, and how do you use it to guide your team or organization?

4. Reflect on the people you lead. What makes them great, and how do you celebrate their contributions to the organization?

5. Describe a time when a leader lacked character or integrity. How did that affect your ability to do your job?

YOUR NEXT STEPS

1. Identify some things you can do to strengthen your most important relationships.

2. Evaluate your organization's objectives and the contributions of those you lead. Plan to have a personal conversation about how you can better empower each person.

3. Plan an event to celebrate a team or organizational accomplishment. A simple "thank-you" lunch might be your best choice.

THE DISCIPLINE OF
GENEROSITY

"REAL GENEROSITY TOWARD THE FUTURE
LIES IN GIVING ALL TO THE PRESENT."
—ALBERT CAMUS

S ome people think generosity is a thing of the past. I disagree. Charitable giving is still strong, even among younger generations. However, people are using different criteria to select charities to give to. They no longer give to their churches just because they were taught to do so; they give to causes that align with their personal values and that do work they think is important.

Young people today are extremely cause-oriented. They want to provide clean drinking water in poor countries and provide food to the most impoverished around the world. They buy products from companies that are actively engaged in alleviating suffering. Some churches suffer financially because their congregations can't identify the causes they are passionate about.

Generosity matters because God's blessings are not meant to flow *to* you; they should flow *through* you. It is the difference between the funnel and the cup. Some people view their lives as cups and look for God to fill them to overflowing. They think that, once they begin overflowing, they will direct the extra to others. But many trade their cups for buckets and their buckets for barrels and their barrels for lakes. They have no intention of letting anything overflow.

> If you are not prepared to be generous, you'll miss out on the blessing of investing in others.

Our lives are not cups, buckets, barrels, or lakes; they are funnels. No matter how little or how much flows to us, we are responsible for directing it toward things that matter to God. Your wisdom as a leader should flow toward those you lead. Your influence should be directed toward situations where you can make a difference.

There are countless examples of people who used the principle of generosity to transform their lives from mediocre to magnificent. By viewing their lives as a funnel, they have cultivated an attitude that God blesses and rewards.

The discipline of generosity is all about taking advantage of the opportunities you have. If you are not prepared to be generous, you'll miss out on the blessing of investing in others. We often hear stories about people who were impulsively generous, but I doubt their generosity lacked intentionality. No, they were prepared to do something when given the chance, and because they were prepared (remember Chapter 3?), they were able to do something most of us only think about.

I recently heard about a lady who decided to celebrate her fifty-fifth birthday in an unusual way. As the day approached, she determined to give her birthday away by doing something for someone she didn't know—every day for the fifty-five days leading up to her birthday. That's almost two months of planned generosity! The joy she experienced was amazing. She walked up behind a stranger at a coffee shop and bought her coffee. She took gift cards to the Armed Forces recruiting station. She delivered flowers to a random office and sent encouraging notes to people she barely knew. She was intentionally generous and successfully gave away her birthday. During that time, she also was the *recipient* of generosity. Without knowing what the woman was doing for others, a friend gave her a gift card to her favorite grocery store. Other people did similar things that caused her to conclude, "You can't out-give God!"

Another remarkable story about the results of generosity comes from the life experience of my wife's father. In 1949, the Kraisses were—to *understate* their situation—a family of modest financial means. Like many others at the time, the Kraisses were adjusting to life following World War II. Fortunately, sixteen-year-old Glenn Kraiss landed a job as a soda jerk (quite a title, isn't it?) at the Walgreens drugstore in his Southside Chicago neighborhood. The job proved to be a providential fit. He had exceptional interpersonal skills, worked hard, and showed promise far beyond making the perfect chocolate malt. And the store manager noticed.

The manager got to know Glenn and discovered that the young man wanted to attend pharmacy school at the University of Illinois. He also discovered Glenn's family couldn't pay his way to college. Although Glenn had applied for college the summer after he graduated high school, two weeks before he was to start, his parents told him he would not be able to attend. The money wasn't there.

Then, one week before he was to start, Glenn received a postcard saying his tuition, room, and board had been paid in full. It was signed by the Walgreens Drug Company. And for the next eight semesters, he received a postcard in the mail, saying the same thing. Glenn earned his undergraduate degree and then graduated from the University of Illinois pharmacy school.

All during college, he worked at Walgreens and eventually decided that, since the company had invested in him, he would commit his professional life to the company. He rose through the ranks over a fifty-year career—from soda jerk to manager to district manager, regional manager, and senior vice president. He spent the last twenty-one years with the company as executive vice president of all store operations.

So, did Walgreens' investment in Glenn pay off for the company? Exponentially! During Glenn's tenure as EVP, the chain nearly quadrupled in store count from 400 stores to over 2,400 and grew from about 1 billion dollars in sales volume to 15 billion dollars in 1998.

Glenn retired in 1999, and I think it is safe to say he easily covered whatever Walgreens invested in his college tuition. My father-in-law never lost sight of how he was helped, and he, in turn, helped others by investing in them so they, too, could reach great heights. He provided full-ride scholarships to many students—including me. He paid for my master's degree and my doctorate. He knew that developing others for work and service strengthens businesses and communities and makes for a better world.

Glenn Kraiss passed away in January 2013 at the age of seventy-nine. He is greatly missed, especially by my family. He had a way of challenging people to dream big and then encouraging them to work to achieve those dreams. He didn't talk about legacy; he just established a legacy by looking for ways to make a difference for his employer and for the world. He lived his life with profound generosity.

God created you to give, love, and serve others. His generosity should inspire us to be willing to give away everything we have and are. That's hard to do in a culture that tells us to hold on to everything we get, but we must develop the ability to release the things God entrusts to us. We can do that when we realize everything belongs to God.

Paul wrote to his young associate, Timothy, these profound words: "For we brought nothing into the world, and we can take nothing out of it" (1 Timothy 6:7). Because we can't take anything with us, we all will eventually give back everything anyway. Someone else will have whatever you are clinging to. That doesn't make it easy for us to release things into the hands of others. We still want to know the things we give will be used according to their intended purposes.

Giving isn't just about giving money. Giving covers every aspect of life. For example, God doesn't give you wisdom so you can keep it for yourself. He entrusts you with wisdom so you can share it with others.

Sometimes generosity takes on an unexpected form. My wife and I believed God wanted us to have a family, but we had no idea He would prompt us toward adoption. The act of adopting is an act of giving. When people adopt, they give a home to a child who might not otherwise have one. Sometimes generosity looks more like an action than a financial contribution.

God creates opportunities for us to be generous, and we must choose to embrace those opportunities. You can compliment a team member or say thank-you to the hotel staff. You get to choose to send a personal note or bless a server with a generous tip.

Generosity has a lot to do with how God designed you. Some people are more prone to extravagant generosity than others, and that's okay. The Bible identifies generosity as one of the spiritual gifts. That doesn't mean the people without that specific gift don't need to be generous; it means there are some people who have the desire and resources to give of themselves in ways that most people don't understand.

> God creates opportunities for us to be generous, and we must choose to embrace those opportunities.

The real challenge in life is developing a generosity radar. We must be on the lookout for opportunities to release God's blessings into the lives of others. God doesn't expect us to address every need we see, but He does expect us to be responsive to needs that align with our availability.

Being rich is all about choices. When you are willing to give up serving your own needs and sacrifice for the benefit of others, you will discover what it means to be rich. There is a big difference between being rich and being wealthy. You might not have wealth, but you can be rich.

In Luke 12:13–21, Jesus told the story of the rich fool. A successful farmer whose land yielded an amazing harvest had so much that his barns wouldn't hold it all. Although he already had grain and supplies to last for years, he decided to tear down his barns and build even bigger ones. He was more concerned about self-preservation than helping others with his abundance. God's words to the man could be said to us: "You fool! This very night your life will be demanded from you. Then who will get what you have prepared for yourself?"

Your abundance—financial, physical, influential, or technical—isn't for your benefit. It is intended for those God has entrusted to you. An attitude of generosity makes all the difference. You probably remember Marley from *A Christmas Carol*. One of his lines sums up the approach many people have to their lives. He said, "I wear the chain I forged in life. . . . I girded it on of my own free will, and of my own free will I wore it." We all wear the chains of the life we choose.

Each of our divine designs was established by the Ultimate Giver for a purpose we might not understand. Generosity is inherent in the character and nature of God, and one of the most famous verses in the Bible, John 3:16, wonderfully reflects this: "For God so loved the world that he gave his one and only Son, that whoever believes in him shall not perish but have eternal life."

When we live out the truth in John 3:16, our culture is transformed, and the truth multiplies and expands. We will experience a shift in our perceptions as we view life through God's eyes. When that happens:

- **You start to recognize the sacrifice and contributions of others.** Our generosity has a way of tuning our eyes so we can see generosity in action. It helps us see the good in people, rather than the bad.

- **You empower others to be generous.** Sometimes it doesn't take much to get something started. I heard about a couple who went into a coffee shop and were told that their coffee was paid for by someone the day before. One customer paid it forward and started a chain reaction that lasted into the next day. People who benefited from one person's generosity had no problem being generous to others.

- **You release others by giving rather than demanding.** This is an important leadership skill in dealing with your team. When you give mercy, forgiveness, encouragement, wisdom, and so forth, those you lead will be inspired to do better work. Attitude is contagious.

- **You set aside the tendency to control people and processes.** Control is the opposite of generosity. You can't exercise generosity and keep your thumb on everything and everyone. Control creates an oppressive atmosphere, but generosity frees people to lean into their divine designs.

What can you do to become a more generous person? Here are some suggestions:[10]

1. **Write down the benefits of being generous.** Generous people say they are happier, healthier, and more satisfied with life than those who don't exercise generosity.

2. **Express gratitude.** When was the last time you counted your blessings? Write down the things you are grateful for, and review the list. When you remember how blessed you are, you will be more generous toward others.

3. **Do something generous.** You don't have to give away your retirement account, but you can do something small. Buy a stranger a cup of coffee or pay for the meal of a family you don't know who are dining at a table near yours.

4. **Make giving a priority.** Commit to giving a percentage of your salary in accordance with the biblical guidelines. When you get paid, write that check first. You might be surprised what you can do with what's left.

5. **Invest in something you are passionate about.** Whether it's drinking water in Africa or childhood education in your neighborhood,

---

10   These eight points are adapted from Joshua Becker, "10 Simple Ways to Become a More Generous Person," posted at http://www. becomingminimalist.com/10-simple-ways-to-become-a-more-generous-person/

pick something and make a small investment of time, money, or both. As you invest in things that matter to you, you'll become more aware of opportunities to invest more.

6. **Invest in someone you know.** Take time to mentor a younger person in his or her professional, spiritual, or academic growth. You don't have to be an expert, just be willing to let the wisdom you have flow into the life of someone who might need encouragement.

7. **Seek out people in need.** There are probably organizations in your community where you can invest in people in need without having to go through the screening process. Serve meals at a homeless shelter, or teach English as a second language. There is something you can do to help people start pursuing their divine designs.

8. **Get to know a generous person.** It might be hard to find a generous person because those who are truly generous don't often brag about their actions. However, in conversations you can learn about people and generally detect a person who is generous.

The discipline of generosity, like the other disciplines, won't invade your life and take over. It takes time and intentionality. The more you focus on being generous, the more you'll discover how generous God has been to you. This is the cycle that cultivates a heart of gratitude and helps keep us humble.

KEY IDEAS

- People give to causes that align with their values and do work they think is important.

- God's generosity should inspire us to be willing to give away everything we have and are.

- We must be on the lookout for opportunities to release God's blessings into the lives of others.

- When you give mercy, forgiveness, encouragement, wisdom, and so forth, those you lead will be inspired to do better work. Attitude is contagious.

- The more you focus on being generous, the more you'll discover how generous God has been to you. This is the cycle that cultivates a heart of gratitude and helps keep us humble.

DISCUSSION QUESTIONS

1. Think about your organization. How do your values align with the values of those you are trying to reach or influence? How do you communicate your values to your target audience?

2. How does your life reflect the amazing generosity God has shown to you?

3. What is your strategy for determining when to give to a need and when not to give?

4. "Attitude is contagious." Take some time to talk
    about how your team or organization reflects
    your attitude.

5. Generosity isn't about money only. What are some
    other ways you can demonstrate generosity?

YOUR NEXT STEPS

1. If you haven't clearly articulated your
    organizational or team values, spend some time
    putting them on paper.

2. Brainstorm a list of ways you can exhibit
    generosity so that it encourages people in their
    relationships with God.

3. Consider targeting a specific organization or
    ministry in which to invest some of your profits.

THE DISCIPLINE OF
LEARNING

"WE ARE WHAT WE REPEATEDLY DO.
EXCELLENCE, THEN, IS NOT AN ACT,
BUT A HABIT."
—*ARISTOTLE*

T hose who refuse to learn are falling behind. Few people would disagree with that statement. Our world is changing faster than any time in history. Every new product seems to have a shorter shelf life than its predecessor, and this holds true for knowledge as well.

The discipline of learning should strengthen over time. Colleges and universities have created degree programs specifically for adult nontraditional students. This trend has come about in response to the increasing number of adults who are returning to school to complete their degrees or change careers.

I understand the importance of learning. I earned my undergraduate degree in broadcast journalism and worked in that field for a season. Through a significant series of events, I felt God's call into ministry and found myself in need of additional education. Specifically, I needed to pursue theological training. The journey toward my divine design provided several learning opportunities, and, today, I find myself continuously learning something new.

My learning hasn't been limited to formal education. I sought out mentors like John Wallace, President of Azusa Pacific University, and Roger Heuser, Professor at Vanguard University. These two men helped me understand the potential for organizations and leading transformational change. And as I explained earlier, my pastor during high school, Fred Cottriel, guided me through the discovery of my divine design. There were also many others who played important roles in my education.

"Formal" and "informal" types of education each play their part. I knew the technical training I received would best prepare me for whatever God had in store. As leaders, we must understand the history of our chosen fields and be well informed about the philosophies and thinkers who played significant roles in the development of our specialty areas. This happens only in formal educational settings.

The human "law of inertia" opposes our desire to learn. We tend to drift toward efficiency rather than effectiveness. As a result, we get very good at what we do, but our peripheral skills diminish. If we aren't intentional about lifelong learning, we will lose our relevance and squander the opportunities God places in front of us.

Once formal training is finished, we must become self-directed learners. No one stands over us, waiting for us to turn in a paper. We don't have to go to class. Learning is totally up to us, so if we aren't intentional about learning, we won't learn. It's that simple. The demands of your job as a leader are ever-changing and, often, ever-increasing. You need a continual process of learning that keeps you at your maximum effectiveness.

When you make growing and learning a priority, you will constantly reevaluate your life and leadership skills. As you do, you will discover aspects of your work that need improvement. These are the areas in which you have the motivation to learn.

Adults learn in response to a real or perceived need. We don't get excited about information for the sake of information. This is an important distinction and something that affects our learning environments. Think, for instance, about how you select books or articles to read or seminars to attend. You might be motivated by a referral, review, or advertisement. There is a good possibility that something you read resonated with a real or perceived need or interest. You most likely didn't purchase a book about something that doesn't interest you.

The same process you go through to select a book or seminar is the same process that drives your learning. There was a reason you picked up this book. That reason reflects your motivation to learn.

> If we aren't intentional about lifelong learning, we will lose our relevance and squander the opportunities God places in front of us.

We must distinguish between the ways children learn and the ways adults learn. Much of childhood education is focused on basic skills. Children learn their numbers, colors, mathematical processes, and language. As they mature, they progress up the cognitive domain and begin manipulating information. Their reasoning skills develop, and they can handle processes that weren't possible when they were children.

From adolescence to adulthood, the reasoning skills sharpen, and the foundations are simply components of the learning process. When we approach adult learning from a childhood learning perspective, we short-circuit the learning process. Adults don't want to sit in rows and be told what to think; they want to use their heads and participate in the process.

> **You'll never be motivated to learn until you have some goals in mind to encourage the learning experience.**

Why is this important? You need to know how you learn, so you can approach self-directed learning from an informed perspective. The discipline of learning is all about growing in knowledge and wisdom. It takes practice and discipline.

You'll never be motivated to learn until you have some goals in mind to encourage the learning experience. Adult educators use the term "cognitive dissonance." This is the gap between what you know and what you need to know. Some adults struggle to embrace the educational process because they haven't clearly identified the gap they are trying to fill.

As a leader, you probably have goals for your team or organization. You understand that you can't make all of the changes immediately. That's why it is important to work backwards from your vision, identifying the sequential steps needed to get there. Your goal is to design a process of manageable changes that can be accomplished over time and that ultimately lead to the realization of the vision.

Once you define the steps, look closely at the *first* step. What do you need to know in order to reach that goal? What resources are available to help you fill the gap? This denotes your motivation to learn. Don't worry about anything else on the list; stick to the first task.

Radio talk show host and financial expert Dave Ramsey talks about the baby steps needed to achieve financial stability. He begins by telling people to save one thousand dollars in an emergency fund and to cut up their credit cards. He then advises them to begin paying off their debts from smallest to largest. He reminds people to focus on paying off the debt and not to get distracted by other financial goals.

Ramsey's plan works in the arena of learning, too. You need to focus on step one in your leadership process and work on it until it is complete. The accomplishment of the initial step will provide the enthusiasm you need to tackle the next steps. Your enthusiasm will drive the learning you need as you go along.

Learning takes on many forms. You can focus on skills development, a spiritual discipline, or a specific aspect of your job. You might need to learn how to use a software program or computer. You might focus on one of the leadership disciplines in this book and devote your attention to its development. There might be a job-related task that you need to become more familiar with.

HOW DO YOU LEARN?

We learn all the time. When you pick up a magazine, newspaper, or tablet device, you learn something. The question is: what are you learning? Are you investing your time in learning that is valuable to your life and your divine design, or are you giving your time to things that aren't significant? If you're a good steward of that learning time, you'll want to choose something that matters. Here are some ways you can become a lifelong learner of things that make a difference:

1. **Read.** Create a reading list based on your perceived needs and interests. Make sure you always have the next resource on hand so you don't give yourself an excuse to not read. Stay informed on trends in your area of expertise. The proliferation of online material makes that a pretty easy task.

2. **Choose a mentor.** Select someone in your field, and ask him or her to meet with you in person or online once every week or two. Respect your mentor's time by being prompt and by having a few questions to ask at every meeting. Most leaders are honored when someone asks them to be a mentor.

3. **Be picky about your friends.** You will become like the people you hang around with. If you are friends with people who have no ambition and are

satisfied with mediocrity, you'll eventually adopt their way of thinking. Choose people who share your passion for life and your commitment to discovering their divine designs.

4. **Listen to podcasts.** This is something great to do when you are in traffic or traveling on business. Look for podcasts from professionals in your areas of expertise. But remember: their podcasts are expressions of their opinions, so don't take everything at face value. Some of their ideas will be good, but some should be taken with a grain of salt.

5. **Attend conferences.** Select one or two conferences per year to attend. The conferences need to be connected to your areas of expertise and to your learning goals.

6. **Stay in communication with those you serve.** Although I'm president of the university, the school exists to serve the community and churches by providing spiritually-grounded, well-prepared graduates. When I understand the market, I can better lead my team and my organization to deliver what the market wants.

7. **Accept challenges.** Don't dismiss opportunities just because they are difficult. Embrace situations that push you out of your comfort zone and force you to learn.

> **Having a fundamental curiosity or appetite for life will keep you learning.**

Having a fundamental curiosity or appetite for life will keep you learning. You don't have to give in to the temptation to settle. Stagnation is one thing that will compromise any leader's ability to lead. By continuing to learn, you will continue to come alive, and your divine design will become increasingly apparent.

As leaders, we must always adapt to new technology. I'm amazed at how many gadgets become obsolete just about the time I learn to use them. But that's the new normal, so we better get used to it. The good thing is that young people understand new technology. When I have questions, I often look to my three children. They have the upper hand when it comes to navigating the latest technology.

Learning will make you a better you. But learning takes time, and that is often one thing we have in limited quantity. Finding ways to manage your time better will open your eyes to learning opportunities and will clear your mind so you can be a better learner. When you cultivate the skill of time management, you will experience one or more of the following results:

1. **It will help you determine your priorities.** Putting things on a schedule forces you to think about their relative importance.

2. **It will change your schedule.** When you track your time, you'll discover some things that interfere with your productivity.

3. **It will help direct your thought life.** When you bring order to your schedule, you organize your thoughts. Eliminating something from the calendar has a way of helping to remove it from your mind.

4. **It will allow time for unexpected things.** Life isn't predictable, so you need to allow some contingency time. Scheduling your events frees up time that can be used for unexpected things or for much-needed down time.

5. **It will shape your convictions.** You'll know what's really important when you look at it on your calendar. Some of the things you have typically given time to might not make the cut.

6. **It will reveal your core values.** The things on your calendar are evidence of your value system. When you take a holistic look at your month, you'll see what you value, and you'll uncover values you don't hold and that you need to get rid of.

Learning doesn't just happen; you must be intentional about pursuing it. The discipline of learning separates real leaders from people who merely fill leadership roles. I've never met a real leader who wasn't a learner.

KEY IDEAS

- Those who refuse to learn are falling behind.

- The human "law of inertia" opposes our desire to learn. We tend to drift toward efficiency rather than effectiveness.

- You'll never be motivated to learn until you have some goals in mind to encourage the learning experience.

- Stagnation will compromise a leader's ability to lead.

- Finding ways to better manage your time will open your eyes to learning opportunities and clear your mind so you can be a better learner.

DISCUSSION QUESTIONS

1. What are some things you are studying or reading about right now? Why are these important to you?

2. How do you evaluate the effectiveness of your leadership and your organization?

3. What are your lifelong learning goals? What do you want to learn in the next year? Five years?

4. When you believe things are as good as they can get, you'll grow stagnant. How do you defend yourself against the tendency toward stagnation?

5. What are some of your most significant time-wasters, and how do you keep yourself from wasting time?

YOUR NEXT STEPS

1. Develop a reading list related to things you want to learn now and in the future.

2. Enroll in an online course or live class that will help you learn something new.

3. Track your use of time over the next days and evaluate it to identify ways you are wasting time.

THE DISCIPLINE OF
OPPORTUNITY

"OPPORTUNITY IS MISSED BY MOST PEOPLE
BECAUSE IT IS DRESSED IN OVERALLS
AND LOOKS LIKE WORK."
—*THOMAS EDISON*

I never could have predicted the journey my life would take. How did a broadcast journalism major become a university president? He didn't. It's not that simple. The broadcaster took the first step, and many steps later, that man became the president of a university. I experienced the discipline of opportunity.

You will be moved into new places of greater influence when you are ready to fulfill God's destiny. You can't set your sights on the ultimate goal without first being committed to your current assignment. I would not be where I am today had I not fulfilled the responsibilities of each opportunity along the way.

Many potential leaders never step into their destinies because they refuse to do the job they've been assigned. Many corporations require aspiring managers to work at every level of the organization before they become managers. Why?

Leaders must understand the path. They need to appreciate the opportunities they have.

How do you recognize *your* opportunities? Not every opportunity that comes along is one on which you should act. Although it's not easy to choose in advance which opportunities are right, you can create a filter through which to consider every option you have. The filter should include considerations like your future hopes and dreams, your moral convictions, your spiritual needs, and your family. Decide in advance what really matters to you, and use those criteria to evaluate any opportunity that comes your way.

> When you stay aware of what could be next, you will resist the natural tendency to grow stagnant and complacent.

Leaders should never get the idea that they have arrived. There is always something more, whether in your current organization or outside of it. When you stay aware of what could be next, you will resist the natural tendency to grow stagnant and complacent. Even if you stay in your present position for the remainder of your years, you'll remain vibrant by keeping your head up.

Geoff Mulgan, chief executive of NESTA, said, "The idea of entrepreneurship applies as much in politics, religion, society and the arts as it does in business." Successful leaders have an entrepreneurial mindset. They recognize an opportunity, capture the moment, and step into it through their divine designs.

The entrepreneurial mindset separates exceptional leaders from average leaders. However, not all organizations are open to the spirit of the entrepreneur. Some are so rooted in their pasts that they can't set leaders free to lead. I've seen this in many organizations but especially in churches.

Years ago when he first went to southern California, Rick Warren was considered by many to be a renegade. Though educated in a traditional environment, his entrepreneurial approach to ministry was controversial. Some people resisted because they always resist anything that doesn't resonate with historical approaches. Others resisted because they didn't want Warren to prove that a different way to do things might not only work but be wildly successful. Some people (very few) cheered him on, and ultimately, Saddleback Church was born and has become a standard bearer and game changer in the church community. The same can be said about other leaders who dared to break away from their pasts and do something different.

The entrepreneurial spirit is the heartbeat of many leaders. They see something others can't see and have a plan to get there. When it comes to leading your team or your organization, you need to have some of the characteristics usually associated with entrepreneurs. Here are five traits to adopt:[11]

1. **Passion.** Effective leaders are motivated by more than simply doing their jobs. There is something intrinsic about what they do. They connect their roles to a greater cause and lead with enthusiasm and vibrancy.

---

11   These five points are adapted from Nathan Resnick, "5 Key Characteristics Every Entrepreneur Should Have," posted at http://www.entrepreneur.com/article/232991.

2. **Perseverance.** Leaders always face obstacles. They understand that change takes time. Effective leaders stick to their plans and keep moving forward while building trust and growing their spheres of influence. As a leader, you must accept the fact that not everyone will agree with your decisions. You must be committed to following through on what you said you would do. If you ever give in to the resistance, you'll find it harder to keep moving forward.

3. **Resourcefulness.** Your divine design is one of your most valuable resources. As a leader, you understand your strengths and how to assemble a team that compensates for your weaknesses. Knowing how to use your available resources prevents you from postponing action until things are better. Many church planters readily acknowledge the limitations of their resources in the early days of their churches. The real test of their leadership ability comes later when those excuses are removed.

4. **Open-mindedness.** Successful leaders must be flexible and willing to make course corrections along the way. Things seldom turn out like you plan—which is fine as long as you have a way to keep the plan moving forward while working around the challenges.

5. **Sponge-like nature.** Leaders are learners. When it comes to taking advantage of the opportunities

in front of you, a willingness to learn will carry you a long way. Be an active learner. Read books and articles. Talk to other leaders. Study business models and marketing plans. Reach outside your chosen field and look for successful leaders. Consider things they've done that you can adapt for your setting.

Your entrepreneurial tendencies will prepare you to recognize and respond to the "aha moments" that come along. First responders live with this sense of expectancy. They are highly trained and completely capable of dealing with emergency situations. When a call comes in, they don't have to think about what to do; they jump into action. Effective leaders have the same attitude. They are prepared to respond to opportunities as they come along. They can't predict when they will act, but they are certain they will respond.

The more prepared you are to respond to opportunities, the more opportunities you will have. It's not magic; it's reality. Why? You probably have missed some opportunities because

The more prepared you are to respond to opportunities, the more opportunities you will have.

you weren't prepared to respond. Your eyes weren't tuned to see the potential. Many leaders approach their responsibilities like tumbleweed. They roll through life, picking up additional responsibilities without letting go of any of the previous responsibilities and miss the best ones that come their way. (This is also how burnout begins!)

In his book, *Die Empty,* Todd Henry recounts a response he received to the question, "What do you think is the most valuable land in the world?" There were many great responses, but the one that stuck with him is worth thinking about. Henry's friend said, "You're all wrong. The most valuable land in the world is the graveyard. In the graveyard are buried all of the unwritten novels, never-launched businesses, un-reconciled relationships, and all of the other things that people thought, 'I'll get around to that tomorrow.' One day, however, their tomorrows ran out."[12]

As a leader, you should cultivate a strong sense of awareness that helps you connect the dots and see opportunities as they develop. The more you do this, the more you will see your God-given divine design in action. God often has a lot more confidence in your ability than you do. He is always willing to guide you into opportunities you don't feel prepared to handle. That's been His mode of operation throughout history.

God sees the future as if it has already happened. Therefore, when He leads you into uncertainty, you are the only one who is uncertain. He already knows where you are going. The struggles we have in leadership often are the result of our passive resistance to God's guidance. Although God is certain, we stall out. We miss the opportunity and settle for the predictable.

I've seen this happen with leaders many times. They choose the complacency of the past over the opportunities of the future. They opt for predictability. There might be an amazing possibility on the horizon, but they miss it because they are looking behind them.

---

12   Todd Henry, *Die Empty: Unleash Your Best Work Every Day* (New York: Penguin Group, 2013), 4.

In Luke 9:62, Jesus said, "No one who puts a hand to the plow and looks back is fit for service in the kingdom of God." Those are strong words every leader should consider. When God says you are ready, you are ready. It doesn't matter what you think. What worked in the past will deliver results you've already experienced. If you want to experience something different, you will have to *do* something different.

I'm surprised by how many leaders believe they can keep doing what they've always done and experience improved results. It doesn't work that way. As a matter of fact, the opposite is true. If you do what you've always done, you will experience ever *decreasing* results. Although leaders who are "stuck" see the decrease happen year after year, they choose to stick

> **If you do what you've always done, you will experience ever *decreasing* results.**

with tradition. They can't explain why some events are on the calendar. All they know is that those events were on the calendar at the same time last year!

You might remember the story of the Israelites' escape from Egypt. Their ultimate destination was the Promised Land (Canaan)—roughly a three-day journey from Egypt. But the land between Egypt and Canaan was occupied by a nation the Israelites would long remember: the Philistines. While bemoaning their situation in Egypt, the Israelites did little to prepare for their future.

You know the story. Moses reluctantly returned from the desert and prepared to take God's people to freedom and the land that had been promised to them. They were ready to go—or were they? In Exodus 13:17–18 we read:

> When Pharaoh let the people go, God did not lead them on the road through the Philistine country, though that was shorter. For God said, "If they face war, they might change their minds and return to Egypt." So God led the people around by the desert road toward the Red Sea.

The Israelites were *not* ready, so God led them on a detour. A journey that should have taken three days took forty years. God's people weren't ready to seize the opportunity before them. An entire generation never saw Canaan because they were not ready to act when God said to act.

This is where faith meets reality. It's easy to say we want to be used by God to do something significant, but are we ready when the opportunity arises? Are we ready to change employers, move to a new city, or change careers? As we look back, we see how God has shaped our paths. If He's done it before, He will do it again.

When you are ready to fulfill God's destiny for your life, the opportunity will come. How will you know you're ready? I discovered that my maturity had to match the moment. God wouldn't give me opportunities I wasn't mature enough to handle. This is true of any of us: you can step into a role, not because you are ready, but because you have maturity and experience to the point where you can be used in that setting.

When that happens, you'll still feel overwhelmed. You will wonder what you have gotten yourself into. At the same time, you'll have the drive and determination to meet the challenges head on. Your divine design will show, and God will be honored.

All coaches have words of wisdom for their teams. Years of personal experience give them what it takes to guide their teams toward championships. You might hear one of them say, "What has gotten me to this position is going to help us win." That is the attitude of a leader.

God creates opportunity. Are you willing to step forward?

KEY IDEAS

- You will be moved into new places of greater influence when you are ready to fulfill God's destiny.

- When it comes to leading your team or your organization, you need to have some of the characteristics usually associated with entrepreneurs.

- The more prepared you are to respond to opportunities, the more opportunities you will have.

- God often has a lot more confidence in your ability than you do. He is always willing to guide you into opportunities you don't feel prepared to handle.

- You can step into a role, not because you are ready, but because you have maturity and experience to the point where you can be used in that setting.

DISCUSSION QUESTIONS

1. What is God's destiny for your life, and how are you preparing for it?

2. What does it mean to be an entrepreneurial leader? In what ways are you empowering those you lead to be entrepreneurs?

3. Describe a time when you stepped into an opportunity for which you were prepared. What role did preparation play in your discovery of that opportunity?

4. Why does God guide us into opportunities we don't feel prepared to handle?

5. Compare your leadership maturity today to what it was a few years ago. Describe your maturation process. In what ways are you continuing to mature as a leader?

YOUR NEXT STEPS

1. Write down in your journal your understanding of God's destiny for your life. Revisit the statements often, and add additional thoughts as they come to mind.

2. Look for ways to make your leadership environment more entrepreneurial.

3. Spend some time reading the book of Proverbs and look for wisdom that will help you be a better leader.

THE DISCIPLINE OF
MISSIONAL LIVING

"OUTSTANDING PEOPLE HAVE ONE THING IN COMMON: AN ABSOLUTE SENSE OF MISSION."

—ZIG ZIGLAR

Successful leaders know who they are and why they exist. Their mission is clear.

A resume stated a candidate's personal mission. He wrote, "I exist to honor God by encouraging and equipping people to fall in love with, study, and apply God's Word to their lives." A sense of mission is the filter through which every opportunity passes.

As a leader, you have the responsibility to maintain a sense of God's purpose in your life. You must respond with intentionality to your calling in every context. This is God's plan for your life; it is your divine design.

Over the course of your life, you will see God's hand guiding you along His path. The opportunities you have should mesh with your sense of mission and purpose. You must be aware of God's purpose for you where you are while maintaining a sense of expectancy for whatever is next.

If you understand your mission, you can be certain you are exactly where you need to be right now. Your mission confirms your decisions and provides context for the consideration of future opportunities.

Understanding your mission requires you to have a sense of your missional design. God didn't leave you here to do whatever you want. He has a mission *for you*. Your mission is different from your job. A job simply provides the context for the employment of your mission. You will probably have numerous jobs throughout your life, and they generally serve to move you along your career path.

> The more clearly you understand your mission, the better prepared you will be to make decisions.

Your mission, though, is also different from your career. A career is your chosen field of study and investment. Many people change careers. A doctor, for instance, might become a missionary. The doctor had a mission to help people thrive physically, and he can do that through a career as a doctor, a missionary, or a number of other options. A person can change careers but never change his or her life mission.

Your missional design allows you to get to the heart of who you really are. What is your passion in life, and how does God want to use you to make Him known? These are the questions that guide the understanding of your mission. The more clearly you understand your mission, the better prepared you will be to make decisions. Things that align with your mission are easy to spot; things that don't align are easy to avoid.

Establishing your mission requires focus. *One Word That Will Change Your Life* by Jon Gordon, Dan Britton, and Jimmy Page is a valuable tool to help focus on one element of your life.[13] I've used their one-word process to help me live within my mission.

In 2011, my one word was *listening.* I was determined to position myself to truly listen to God, my family, colleagues, and so forth. I wanted to listen to the quietness. Listening was important because there were so many things in my life that needed God's direction and clarity. Out of that process came some of the critical mission objectives that are a part of my life today.

In 2012, my words were *courage* and *conviction.* People who live with courage and conviction will see God do great things. The Bible is full of stories of people who had conviction and who took action. Paul faced hostile situations, yet he never backed down. Jesus was stalked by the Pharisees and knew their power but stuck to His convictions. Shadrach, Meshach, and Abednego stood up to Nebuchadnezzar while realizing the king had the power to put them to death. The more I focused on courage and conviction, the more those qualities developed in my life.

Then, 2013 was my year of *intentional living.* Everyone lives, but how many people live with a sense of purpose? This was the question that motivated me to be more intentional. It required a keen sense of awareness and purpose. I couldn't go through the motions of just doing life; I had to ascertain the value of the things I was doing. During this time, I gave a coin to each student I mentored at Southeastern. Two words were

---

13   Jon Gordon, Dan Britton, and Jimmy Page, *One Word That Will Change Your Life* (Hoboken, NJ: Wiley, 2012).

inscribed on the coin: intentional living. I told students to give coins to the person in whom they would invest themselves. That process was an eye-opener for many of them. Few of us really have that sense of intentionality. Even fewer are willing to lock in their commitments with action.

Having a sense of mission will guide your conversations, your leadership activities, and your spontaneous interactions. A sense of mission won't, however, find you. It requires determination and resolve, so here are some things you can do to identify your sense of mission:

1. **Pay attention to the moments you have each day.** Everyone is in a hurry. We have this idea that we can multitask, but our brains lack the ability to pay full attention to more than one thing at a time. The busier we are, the less likely we are to see needs around us. One day, I was in the café between meetings and noticed a student who looked like he needed some encouragement. I took a moment to speak to him and later found out that my sensitivity was really a divine appointment. That student needed what I had to offer.

2. **Pay attention to the people in your life.** Business robs us of spontaneity. We get focused on what we have to do next and where we need to be. It's easy to overlook family members, coworkers, delivery people, and so forth. Even when we find time to share with others, our minds can be a million miles away. Being physically

present without being mentally present is relationally counterproductive. Look for ways to show kindness. Let someone get ahead of you in the grocery line. Offer to return a shopping cart for a mom dealing with her children. Go out of your way to be nice to people, and you'll be surprised what happens.

3. **Pay attention to the whispers of God.**
   Take time to listen to His still, small, guiding voice. Respond to the invitation Jesus gave to His disciples and that I believe He gives to all of us. Mark 6:31 is one of my favorite verses in the Bible. Jesus said, "Come with me by yourselves to a quiet place and get some rest." You want to make more room for the voice of God in your life, but you can so easily drown out that voice with noise, distractions, and busyness. And before you know it, another day has passed and you haven't given God any space, any room. I do wonder how many of God's whispers I have missed. In Mark 6, Jesus and the disciples planned to go away to get some rest. The crowd that followed Him, however, had other plans. Jesus eventually found Himself surrounded by at least five thousand men. Some commentators estimate that the crowd numbered in excess of fifteen thousand when counting the women and children. Jesus could have turned them away, but He viewed them through His mission. The miracle of the feeding

of the five thousand was a direct result of Jesus' understanding of His purpose and mission.

On the first day of a college seminar he was giving, Professor Tony Campolo stepped around to the front of his desk, looked at his students, and asked them the question: "How long have you lived?"

No one answered. So he pointed to one young man—looked right at him—and said, "Young man, how long have you lived?"

The student responded instinctively, "Twenty-four years."

"No, no," Tony replied. "I didn't ask how long you have existed as a breathing, functioning member of the human race; I wanted you to tell me how long you have really been alive."

And then Tony told the story about how when he was twelve-years-old, he got to go to the top of the Empire State Building in New York City, which used to be a really big deal. He described his intense awareness of that experience, saying that "in a mystical way, I stepped outside myself in that moment and I reflected upon myself experiencing it." He said,

> You're not going to live the way God wants you to live until you build habits that help you discern how to be fully alive.

"I don't know how long I will live, but if I live for a million years, I would remember that moment because I really *lived* it."

Then he said, "Now, young man, let me ask you the question again. How long have you lived?"

And the young man said, "Maybe a minute. Maybe two."[14]

You're not going to live the way God wants you to live until you build habits that help you discern how to be fully alive. In his book *Put Your Dream to the Test,* John Maxwell identifies ten questions to guide your thinking and contextualize your vision.[15] For leaders, his questions can be adapted as follows:

1. **Are you living your divine design, or have you borrowed someone else's?** This might sound silly, but too many people try to replicate what they see others doing. God didn't create you to be an imitation of someone else; He created you to be you.

2. **Do you clearly see your divine design?** Do you understand how you are put together and the amazing strengths God has placed inside you? When you do, you'll be better able to rest in who you are while encouraging others to be their best, too.

3. **Are you disciplined?** Effective leaders have a clear understanding of their tendency to waste the resources God has entrusted to them. Because of that, they have a strategy in place to help them become more effective by limiting the distractions.

14   Tony Campolo, *Let Me Tell You a Story* (Nashville, TN: Thomas Nelson, 2000), 72.

15   John C. Maxwell, *Put Your Dream to the Test* (Nashville, TN: Thomas Nelson, 2011).

4. **Does your divine design motivate you to embrace it?** If not, it's not your divine design. When you understand how God has put you together, you will seek to live it out in your everyday life.

5. **Do you have a plan to be the best leader you can be?** You can't rely on what you've done in the past. You must be willing to learn from others, listen to criticism, make course corrections, and live with integrity.

6. **Are you encouraging the people you lead?** There is no place for arrogance in leadership. If it weren't for God's grace, you wouldn't be in the position you are in. Express your gratitude to God daily and maintain a humble approach to life. As you do, you will be an encouragement to everyone around you, and you will attract the best talent available.

7. **Are you willing to pay the price for being the leader?** This means taking responsibility for those you lead without throwing others under the bus. It also means setting aside any competitive nature and desire to be the king of the hill. Are you willing to work harder than anyone on the team or in the organization?

8. **Are you making progress as a leader?** Are you a better leader today than you were last month or last year? What would those you lead say about

your leadership skills? It's easy to give yourself a passing grade. After all, you know how hard you've worked and what you do each day. Those you lead, however, might see things differently. In the words of Andy Stanley, "What's it like to be on the other side of me?"

9. **Are you satisfied in your role as a leader?** This is a big question because many leaders are promoted to their level of incompetence. If you aren't feeling a sense of satisfaction, dig to the bottom of the situation and decide whether you are living in your divine design or not.

10. **Am I a benefit to others?** Ultimately, leadership is all about those you influence. If you aren't a benefit to others, you are a drain on them. Leaders need to evaluate their effects on other people and see if they are being jerks or not.

You can never take credit for your life as a leader. God designed you for a specific task and prepared you along the way. Though you have gifts and abilities, He is the One who gave them to you. The more you recognize that, the better you will be at living within your divine design.

I haven't mastered all of this. In fact, I have a long way to go, but I understand God is doing a work in and through me. Just writing that humbles me. The Creator of the universe cares enough about me to design me for a responsibility that brings me great joy and Him great honor. He breathed into me the skills and abilities I need to succeed. He nurtures them through the resources and people He brings into my life. His grace and love are woven through every part of my existence.

It would be easy to take credit for what has happened in my life except that I'm not smart enough to make all of the details work out. I couldn't have designed this path, nor can you design yours. I never saw this coming, but God always saw it. Though I might be surprised, He never is.

I don't deserve anything He has given me, but He deserves everything I have. God is good. That's why I discipline myself to be a good steward of the life He gave me. Scripture teaches that one day I will stand before God and give an account of how I fulfilled the mission He designed for me.

In his book *Chazown,* Craig Groeschel shares the story of what happened at the 2004 summer Olympics with the American athlete Matthew Emmons. On track for the gold in the fifty-meter, three-position rifle final, Emmons was up for his final shot. He was so far ahead of the other competitors that all he had to do was send a bullet anywhere through the inner ring of the target to seal his gold medal. He prepared himself mentally. He paused his breathing. He took aim. Then he fired. The bullet passed right through the bull's-eye, but he was puzzled when the tone indicating a hit didn't sound. Emmons then realized that the bull's-eye he had hit was on the wrong target! He dropped from first place, and a virtually guaranteed gold medal, to eighth. The right shot hit the wrong target.[16]

One day you'll stand before a greater judge than any who has officiated at the Olympics. What will you say if He tells you

16   Craig Groeschel, *Chazown: Define Your Vision. Pursue Your Passion. Live Your Life on Purpose* (Colorado Springs, CO: Multnomah, 2010), 26.

that, in your life, you hit the wrong target? What if He says you weren't a good steward of His divine design? For those questions, you'll want to make sure you have the right answers.

KEY IDEAS

- Successful leaders know who they are and why they exist.

- Having a sense of mission will guide your conversations, your leadership activities, and your spontaneous interactions.

- You're not going to live the way God wants you to live until you build habits that will help you discern how to be fully alive.

- You can never take credit for your life as a leader. God designed you for a specific task and prepared you along the way.

- I don't deserve anything He has given me, but He deserves everything I have. God is good.

DISCUSSION QUESTIONS

1. Why do you think God designated you as a leader? What unique qualities do you have that position you for leadership success?

2. How would you describe your sense of mission? How does a sense of mission influence your leadership decisions?

3. What does being fully alive mean to you? How are you pursuing it?

4. In what ways does your life help others understand more about who God is?

5. Your life reveals your real relationship with God. What does your daily living say about the quality of your spiritual life?

YOUR NEXT STEPS

1. Identify and write down your mission statement. Discuss the mission statement with other organizational leaders.

2. Look for evidence that you are fully alive. Schedule time to do something that encourages your creativity.

3. Study biblical leadership and look for ways to incorporate biblical principles into your life.

APPENDICES

Appendix 1

JOURNAL EXERCISE

In the space provided, write down your personal thoughts about each chapter. For each chapter, ask the following questions:

- What did I learn?
- Why is this important to me?
- What will I do in response to what I learned?
- How will this action improve my leadership ability?

CHAPTER 1

The Discipline of Self-Awareness

_____

_____

_____

_____

_____

_____

_____

_____

_____

_____

_____

_____

_____

_____

_____

_____

_____

_____

_____

_____

_____

_____

_____

_____

_____

CHAPTER 2
The Discipline of Self-Management

CHAPTER 3

The Discipline of Self-Preparedness

_____

_____

_____

_____

_____

_____

_____

_____

_____

_____

_____

_____

_____

_____

_____

_____

_____

_____

_____

_____

_____

_____

_____

CHAPTER 4

The Discipline of Character

_____

_____

_____

_____

_____

_____

_____

_____

_____

_____

_____

_____

_____

_____

_____

_____

_____

_____

_____

_____

_____

_____

_____

_____

CHAPTER 5

The Discipline of Relationships

_____

_____

_____

_____

_____

_____

_____

_____

_____

_____

_____

_____

_____

_____

_____

_____

_____

_____

_____

_____

_____

_____

_____

_____

_____

_____

_____

CHAPTER 6
The Discipline of Generosity

_____

_____

_____

_____

_____

_____

_____

_____

_____

_____

_____

_____

_____

_____

_____

_____

_____

_____

_____

_____

_____

_____

_____

_____

CHAPTER 7

The Discipline of Learning

_____

_____

_____

_____

_____

_____

_____

_____

_____

_____

_____

_____

_____

_____

_____

_____

_____

_____

_____

_____

_____

CHAPTER 8

The Discipline of Opportunity

_____

_____

_____

_____

_____

_____

_____

_____

_____

_____

_____

_____

_____

_____

_____

_____

_____

_____

_____

_____

_____

_____

_____

CHAPTER 9

The Discipline of Missional Living

_____

_____

_____

_____

_____

_____

_____

_____

_____

_____

_____

_____

_____

_____

_____

_____

_____

_____

_____

_____

_____

_____

_____

_____

Appendix 2

SCRIPTURE REFERENCES

RECOMMENDED READING

Good to Great: Why Some Companies Make the Leap and Others Don't (Jim Collins)

Primal Leadership: Learning to Lead with Emotional Intelligence (Daniel Goleman, Richard Boyatzis, and Annie McKee)

Influencer: The New Science of Leading Change, Second Edition. (Joseph Grenny, Kerry Patterson, David Maxfield, Ron McMillan, and Al Switzler)

Die Empty: Unleash Your Best Work Every Day (Todd Henry)

The ONE Thing: The Surprisingly Simple Truth Behind Extraordinary Results (Gary Keller and Jay Papasan)

Leading Change: Why Transformation Efforts Fail (John Kotter)

The Leadership Challenge: How to Make Extraordinary Things Happen in Organizations (James M. Kouzes and Barry Z. Posner)

How Successful People Think: Change Your Thinking, Change Your Life (John C. Maxwell)

The 21 Irrefutable Laws of Leadership: Follow Them and People Will Follow You (John C. Maxwell)

Put Your Dream to the Test: 10 Questions that Will Help You See It and Seize It (John C. Maxwell)

Sometimes You Win—Sometimes You Learn: Life's Greatest Lessons Are Gained from Our Losses (John C. Maxwell)

No More Dreaded Mondays: Ignite Your Passion and Other Revolutionary Ways to Discover Your True Calling (Dan Miller)

Wisdom Meets Passion (Dan Miller)

Entreleadership (Dave Ramsey)

Eat Move Sleep: How Small Choices Lead to Big Changes (Tom Rath)

Strengths Based Leadership: Great Leaders, Teams, and Why People Follow (Tom Rath and Barrie Conchie)

Wellbeing: The Five Essential Elements (Tom Rath and James K. Harter)

Leaders Eat Last: Why Some Teams Pull Together and Others Don't (Simon Sinek)

Start with Why: How Great Leaders Inspire Everyone to Take Action (Simon Sinek)

Multipliers: How the Best Leaders Make Everyone Smarter (Liz Wizeman)

ABOUT THE AUTHOR

On February 1, 2011, Dr. Kent Ingle began serving as Southeastern University's fifteenth president. Before becoming SEU's president, Dr. Ingle served as the dean of the College of Ministry at Northwest University in Kirkland, Washington.

Dr. Ingle's professional ministry experience included eight years as a college professor and fifteen years of pastoral leadership to two congregations—one in Los Angeles and the other in Chicago.

Prior to entering professional ministry, Dr. Ingle spent ten years as a television sports anchor for NBC and CBS. He started as an anchor at the age of eighteen in Bakersfield, California, and finished his career in Los Angeles. He covered many professional sports teams and interviewed hundreds of notable people in the professional sports world, including Michael Jordan, Magic Johnson, Kareem Abdul-Jabbar, Pete Rose, Muhammad Ali, and Carl Lewis.

An ordained Assemblies of God minister since 1988, Dr. Ingle earned a Bachelor of Arts degree in broadcast journalism from Vanguard University of Southern California and later completed his Master of Theological Studies at Vanguard. He received his Doctor of Ministry degree from the Assemblies of God Theological Seminary in Springfield, Missouri.

Dr. Ingle has served as Presbyter of the Central Coast Section of the Southern California Assemblies of God, as well as on the boards of several Assemblies of God and para-church organizations. He is a church coach/consultant and a conference speaker.

A California native, Dr. Ingle and his wife, Karen, reside in Lakeland, Florida, and have three teenage children: Davis, Kaila, and Paxton. The family also has two dogs, Lexi and Zoe. Dr. Ingle loves to cycle, run, lift weights, play basketball, and stay as active as possible. When he has down time, you can find him reading books on leadership or watching NBA League Pass.

To contact Dr. Kent Ingle visit www.kentingle.com.

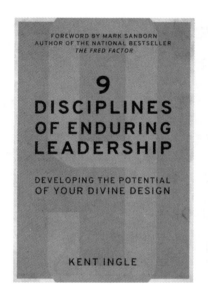

FOREWORD BY MARK SANBORN
AUTHOR OF THE NATIONAL BESTSELLER
THE FRED FACTOR

9 DISCIPLINES OF ENDURING LEADERSHIP

DEVELOPING THE POTENTIAL
OF YOUR DIVINE DESIGN

KENT INGLE

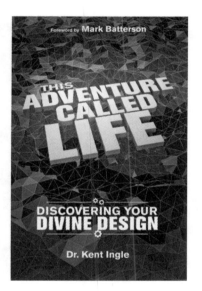

Foreword by **Mark Batterson**

THIS ADVENTURE CALLED LIFE

DISCOVERING YOUR DIVINE DESIGN

Dr. Kent Ingle

FOR MORE INFORMATION ABOUT THESE RESOURCES VISIT

www.influenceresources.com